A GARDENER'S GUIDE TO

PROTECTED GROWING

Creating a successful, sustainable and healthy micro-climate in the garden

A GARDENER'S GUIDE TO PROTECTED GROWING

Creating a successful, sustainable and healthy micro-climate in the garden

GUY DEAKINS

THE CROWOOD PRESS

First published in 2022 by
The Crowood Press Ltd
Ramsbury, Marlborough
Wiltshire SN8 2HR

enquiries@crowood.com
www.crowood.com

British Library Cataloguing-in-Publication Data
A catalogue record for this book is available from the British Library.

ISBN 978 0 7198 4035 7

Dedication
To all my teachers, most especially Magdalen, Zachariah and Matilda. Thank you.

Credits
Dennis Brown, Wikimedia CC (page 65); Ellen Penstone-Smith, Farringford Estate Ltd (pages 33 top and 84); Emil Schneider, Bottle Farm Ltd (page 96); English Heritage (page 9); Gary Todd. Wikimedia CC (page 8); James Goddard, Steelscapes Ltd (page 17); Marie Hourigan (page 80 bottom left and 90); Marshall Space Flight Centre, NASA (page 64 bottom); Michal Klajban, Wikimedia CC (page 85 top); NASA (page 85 bottom right); Peter Trimming, Wikimedia CC (page 88); Phil Rowell, Wikimedia CC (page 22); Ronnie Robertson (page 37); Stephen Boisvert, Wikimedia CC (page 98 top); US National Archives (page 98 bottom); Zero Carbon Farms/Growing Underground (pages 63 bottom and 64 top)

Typeset and designed by D & N Publishing, Baydon, Wiltshire
Cover design by Blue Sunflower Creative
Printed and bound in India by Parksons Graphics

CONTENTS

INTRODUCTION

> 'In the grandest days at Chatsworth, when the sixth Duke of Devonshire was Sultan and Joseph Paxton Grand Vizier of the most ambitious floral court in the world, there were at least forty-five different glass-houses there in addition to the ordinary greenhouses and frames. None was small, and the largest, Paxton's Grand Conservatory, covered an acre of ground, was heated by six miles of pipes and 350 tonnes of fuel a year and upwards of 70,000 feet of glass were needed for glazing the roofs alone.'
>
> M. Tyler-Whittle, *Common or Garden* (1969)

This volume is intended to be strictly utilitarian in its purpose. It has been written in order to supply the gardener (whether professional or amateur) with the best knowledge gleaned from a history of humankind's attempts at creating a microclimate via protective growing.

It covers shelters and screens, structures and tunnels, cultivation and soil, light constraints, temperature control and the importance of sustainability, as well as the vitally important issues of health and hygiene, pest and disease and using allies in the garden. Interspersed throughout the book are points of view from notable amateurs and professionals answering common questions or offering hard-won titbits of information that a horticulturist might find useful in their endeavours (my thanks to the contributors from Kew, Glasnevin, Farringford, Tropical Britain, Audley End House, Kent Wildlife Trust, Howard Nursery, Westland Horticulture, Alitex, Kent Sectional, Polycrub and Steelscapes).

Why Protective Growing?

A garden does not necessarily need a protected environment in the form of a screen, fence or the more specialized environments, such as greenhouses. You can instead use plants that are hardy to your specific climate, buy in plants that need a warm start (sometimes the more economic option, especially if you employ a gardener to tend to them) or grow seasonal vegetables that will take a more exposed location. Take into consideration that glass can be expensive to buy and expensive to upkeep or that hedges take a while to establish plus need to be carefully maintained, and the whole process could be not worth your while. Notwithstanding, the pleasure and reward – once the right conditions have been achieved – are second to none.

To indulge the keen historian, one needs a cursory look at history to whet the appetite further. The concept of protective growing has been long and varied. You will find that most books refer to the Romans as being the first culture to have experimented with the idea of protective growing in the form of greenhouse-like structures in Herculaneum and Pompeii (the Specularia derived its name from *Lapis specularis* – a transparent stone), not forgetting the experiments on the isle of Capri to supply an Emperor with year-round cucumbers. This is wrong. Not only does this view negate any such experimentation with regards to thorn belts – the intentional construction of windbreaks in order to protect crops, or livestock from harm – but it also removes important developments made by previous civilizations. Indeed, it would be remiss of any such book to ignore the developments of the ancient cities of Uruk, Sumer and Ur – the gardens of which were first developed at the insistence of the womenfolk to create protected environments. If one looks further and recognizes the Hanging Gardens at Babylon as another protected construct, again something built at the insistence of a woman (a queen no less), who no doubt wanted her gardeners to grow fruits, flowers and vegetables otherwise unsuited to the heat of the Middle East. Jump ahead a few millennia to the Saxon use of the 'dead-hedge' or *haga*, made from either a simple ditch and mound of stones or stakes of green hawthorn driven into the ground and woven into an impenetrable fence using pliant hazel for strength – protecting the homestead from animal predators and human marauders. These *haga* formed a boundary, a sometimes-living screen that offered a longer term solution to those that had to be maintained and rebuilt, year on year. A few centuries later, the walled gardens of the monastery or, later still, the heated gardens of Renaissance princes are inventions that can be attributed in no small way to the courtyard experiments of much earlier times.

Far Eastern cultures were somewhat more advanced than their European counterparts. Whilst there is no doubt that protective growing was practised, it was not limited to available earth, stone or living materials.

Garden of Nineveh 645–635BCE. Lush gardens, stocked with fruiting plants from many parts of Asia were a common feature of Assyrian palaces.

Audley End House. The restored walled garden provides exceptional shelter both to the glasshouses and food crops grown outside in the changeable East Anglian climate.

According to manuscripts written at the time, the Koreans had fully functioning temperature-controlled glasshouses in the fifteenth century – something that took the Europeans another three centuries to do. However, their ingenuity is not being dismissed to one event here – notable experiments in northern China include interesting results that will be discussed later in this book.

Trials with glass on ways of protecting plants from late frosts, according to European tradition, began in Italy in the fourteenth century. These ideas advanced across Europe to be mentioned in the sixteenth-century book by Thomas Hill, *The Gardener's Labyrinth* (originally published 1577), giving garden historians the first glimpse into the mind of 'simple gardeners' going about their business.

However, the truly great strides in garden ingenuity came after the Industrial Revolution and the advances of iron-making in 1770. That is a time when the names Bonaparte, Paxton and Cocking became synonymous with the pioneering and inventive spirit that was the Enlightenment followed by the Victorian-era garden. Add to that the wealth of plants being brought back by the teams of plant hunters that crossed the globe in ever increasing numbers, it is no wonder Europe continued to push the boundaries of what could be achieved. Stride into the twentieth century and one sees an almost endless series of advances from the replacement of silicate-made glass by wood, plastic, polycarbonate and even aluminium alloy; to the use of passive solar heating, hydroponics and low-energy artificial light to replace the sun!

CHAPTER 1

SHELTERS AND SCREENS

'Our England is a garden and such gardens are not made by singing – "Oh how beautiful", and sitting in the shade. While better men than we go out and start their working lives, at grubbing weeds from gravel-paths with broken dinner knives.'

Rudyard Kipling, *The Glory of the Garden* (1911)

Shelter

In her book, *Seaside Gardening* (1962), Christine Kelway says on the effects of wind:

> Gardeners have little idea how powerful is the effect of wind on the growth of plants. Though the wind maintains a free circulation of air, dispersing excessive humidity and assisting the sun to ripen seed and young wood, it is extraordinarily unkind to plant life.

It is, therefore, in the interests of all gardeners, no matter their situation, to provide as much shelter from desiccating winds as possible. It is all very well for Derek Jarman to have romantically stated, 'There are no walls or fences. My garden's boundaries are the horizon', (from his diary, published in *Modern Nature* 1991 and subsequently used as the title of a major exhibition of his work at the Garden Museum, Lambeth

Derek Jarman Exhibtion. Garden Museum 2020. His 'open' garden withstood one of the harshest climates, but his planting palette was much restricted.

2020). Even he admitted that a gorse hedge would have suited the situation well to provide some shelter. Beautiful though his garden is at Dungeness, his planting palette was drastically reduced to the hardiest of plants.

Taking this as your first lesson, in order to identify threats from the natural environment correctly, first look to see where the prevailing winds come from. This is easily done if you look at the shape of local trees. If exposed to strong winds they will grow in a particular way, the exposed side becoming more aerodynamic, often growing away from the buffeting. Another method is to look at local woodlands or mature hedgerows, if one is nearby. The trees most exposed to high winds will have thicker trunks than those less exposed. This is the side your garden will need protection from the most. The predominant wind in the UK is from the south-west, but if you are on the more exposed eastern side, you may need a north or north-easterly screen too.

Prevailing winds can be harsh. This tree on the South Downs at Chanctonbury is obviously affected by 'Westerlies' moving from left to right of the image.

You will also need to decide what form of shelter you need for your purposes. A hedge or fence is ideal if you are simply aiming to slow the worst of the weather – but choose wisely. A brick wall or concrete fence is ideal if you want to grow trained fruit and retain some heat. A greenhouse, polytunnel or lean-to glass is the next level – but that will need protection itself! Above all, consider your budget and the limitations of space.

Ask an Expert

What are the basic tenets of working within an historic walled garden?

- Making use of the walls for their intended purpose (creating a microclimate) – retaining heat for longer/more efficient cropping and growing trained fruit trees.
- Cyclical seasonal maintenance of annual crops, including successional sowings and trained fruit-tree upkeep, e.g. pruning, feeding and mulching.
- Ensuring that the most appropriate crops are grown according to aspect (south-facing wall, north wall, etc.).
- Making use of glasshouses, some of them heated, where the growing season can be extended and exotic species of fruit and vegetables can be produced, especially historically, e.g. peaches, pineapples and grapevines.
- Crop rotation in the vegetable garden.
- Using traditional Victorian techniques, where possible.
- Putting on a show for our visiting public, e.g. full attractive vegetable plots, herbaceous borders (cut flowers), iris and peony border, in an historic setting.
- Using 'heritage' varieties, where available/appropriate.
- Growing productively for our local vegetable box outlets (Cambridge organic: https://www.cofco.co.uk/ and Nourish Linton: https://nourishlinton.com/).

Kelly Fowler, Senior Kitchen Gardener at Audley End House, English Heritage

The walled garden, Bishops Palace, Fulham. A fine example of a garden designed purely for protective growing.

Inheriting an Existing Shelter

Audley End, near Saffron Walden in Essex, is an interesting historical garden. First laid out in 1605, the house and gardens have seen many changes over the years. One striking feature (among many) is the restored kitchen garden, which has been worked for many centuries and is now run on an entirely organic ethos by English Heritage.

Something often overlooked is what is already there. Whether your space has an existing structure, hedge, treeline or is open to everything, it already has a microclimate. It is worth bearing in mind that all the plants in that space will be growing in that created environment, with that climate as its 'norm'. Assess what benefits the existing situation has and if structural change will be of detriment to the established microclimate. Perhaps a hedge is overgrown or a wall is badly damaged and needs demolishing? If you have plants in the garden that are tender or require specific growing conditions, understand the threat of creating a new microclimate by lowering or removing what is already there. The same goes with new introductions to the space that may create possible frost pockets and wind tunnels or block a natural run-off. Soil damage is also a major consideration when using machinery.

The rule of thumb is to think carefully before creation.

The walled garden at Mount Ephraim, Kent. This garden combines a high wall with a high hedge to create a microclimate.

Artificial Shelter

The Wall

Attractive and long-lived, a well-built wall can be a positive in any garden. Undeniably, it is a very versatile structure if used correctly – it being most suitable to grow fruit trees against, ideal for lean-to structures or walled gardens.

In the book *The Gardener's Assistant* by William Watson (1925), the author describes a wall of six or seven feet (*c.* 2m) as being 'adequate' but '15 feet [4.5m] or more in height would certainly prove very advantageous'. Unless the gardener has no local byelaws to contend with, this idea is pretty impractical in both scope and the majority of budgets. There is also the disadvantage that a wall only fully protects those in the direct lee of its shelter.

However, before it is dismissed out of hand, a good garden wall does have the advantage of being both a shelter and a heat sink. A professional should always be consulted when building a wall of any substance but should an amateur wish an attempt – any description of how is beyond the realms of this book – it is a requirement to check government rules and regulations concerning permanent brick or stone structures and to consult the local buildings' officer.

If you have inherited a wall, then it is wise to inspect the structure and to take remedial action if any of the following is found:

- Is the mortar crumbling and requires re-pointing?
- Is the brickwork damaged, crumbling or cracked?
- Is there a tree nearby that may be causing issues with footings?
- Is the wall thick enough for its height?
- Is the wall upright?
- Has the wall been damaged by climbing plants?
- Is it listed or in a conservation area, requiring specialist treatment?

It is also advisable to assess whether the following conditions have changed since the wall was built:

- Have any large trees been felled nearby causing soil damage?
- Has the wall come into contact with any vehicles?
- Have any supporting structures been removed thereby changing wind load?

After inspection, assess whether it is viable for current *and* future conditions, including wind load and other aspects that you intend the wall to be used for. If at any time the local conditions change, reassess.

Be Aware!

Whilst there are many professionals, both in print and online, giving instructions, liability is always with the builder and owner. Future climate models predict much stronger winds, more frequently, so all walls should be built accordingly.

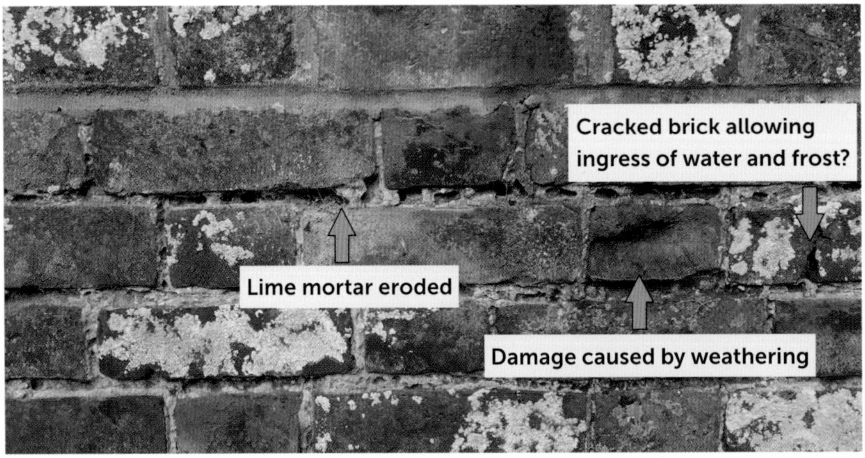

Brick walls are robust but will degrade with weathering and damage.

Another factor to consider is the integrity of the wall structure.

This low wall with ornate metal railings still offers protection, especially as it is so close to the warm house. Private residence.

Gabions

A viable alternative to a brick wall is gabions. In the majority of cases – within the garden setting – gabions are used to shore up slopes. However, used with consideration and creativity, gabions can provide a sturdy and easily created protective barrier if there is space in the garden and the aesthetic is suitable.

Concrete Fence

To many, this is strictly utilitarian and ugly in appearance. However, it does have its merits. Long-lasting and sturdy, it provides an excellent shelter for plants. By its very nature, a south- or west-facing concrete wall acts as an excellent heat sink, absorbing the sun's energy much as the concrete does in a domestic storage-heater, releasing it slowly at night. If used with thought, a concrete fence can be most useful when a glass or plastic structure is built directly adjacent, providing warmth for crops.

Wooden Fence

Cheaper than brick, breeze block or concrete, a wooden fence has the advantage of being easily installed and easily repaired. However, they are lightweight. In urban settings, they are adequate at providing a demarcation between adjoining properties and are most often used for privacy. Rarely do they provide any real protection from the worst of the winter weather and could create a wind-tunnel effect, making things worse. By far the best design is the slatted type, which allows some movement of air without presenting a solid barrier. Fences are not difficult to install, but they are a two-person job – assuming you have the correct digging tools. A brief checklist for installation is as follows:

- Always make sure the workmen use treated timber and that it has a fifteen-year guarantee.
- Make sure the footings are to a correct depth and the uprights are installed using a spirit level. Whether using concrete or wood, 70cm is more than adequate to keep them from being knocked over by a strong wind.
- Check all panels for damage or incorrect manufacture before purchase and again later, before installation.

If you have inherited a wooden fence, check the 'neck' of the uprights around the soil – this is where rot most often takes place. Apply a gentle, but purposeful pressure to the upright, if it moves then it will need replacing soon. Check all the wooden panels for damage, looseness or rot. An application of wood treatment can be applied; if you are in anyway concerned consult a qualified professional.

Hurdles

Hurdles come in two distinct types. The semi-permanent is fixed in place using hardwood staves; this type is an attractive shelter for a newly planted or a sapling protective screen. The second type is a moveable screen, useful around the garden in times of need to protect delicate vegetables or flowers from the worst summer storms. Made from split hazel or osier (willow), they come in varying sizes ready-made or can be created *in situ* by a skilled craftsman. The key to this type of barrier is the upright – always use a hardwood, such as sweet chestnut, in order to ensure that the structure has longevity in the ground and can withstand stronger winds. They are not designed to stop the wind, but to reduce the wind by about 50 per cent, thus they allow the plants to acclimatize to their new environment, without constant buffeting.

An interesting development, and a viable longer-lasting alternative to the traditional wooden hurdle, is to use metal such as those built by Steelscapes in Norfolk, UK. James Goddard, the Managing Director explains:

Hurdles are an excellent and sustainable resource in the garden setting and can be put to use as a screen, as protection for new plantings or simply as a border guard to prevent pedestrian incursion! Private garden.

Steel has many benefits, corten steel in particular – from which the panels are made – has an extremely long life, once the rust layer has formed. Woven steel, 3mm thick, coupled with 6mm mild steel posts provides a very attractive fence with a life well in excess of 25 years, with every aspect fully recyclable. The weave in the fencing will allow some wind to pass through with a porosity of around 65–75 per cent. Filtering the wind results in a more stable microclimate reducing the plants' rate of transpiration and thus dependence on water and stress.... It's worth noting that the weave and robust nature of woven steel fencing means it provides an excellent support for climbers and the advantages that these can bring, such as providing further filtration of the wind but also of noise and air pollution.

(Personal communication, July 2020)

Plastic Windbreak

This 'windbreak' is made from oil-based plastic. They are durable, light and easily moved, coming in rolls of varying length and height. Their use in commercial horticulture – to fill gaps in hedge-lines – is commonplace. However, weathering degrades their properties over a remarkably short time.

Living Shelter Belts

A living shelter belt is commonly known as a hedge or treeline. It is designed to disrupt the worst weather from molesting your garden, orchard, crops or structure. It also has the added bonus, if chosen wisely, of being a roost or shelter for bats (such as the lesser horseshoe), predatory birds (such as robins and thrushes) and insects (such as the scorpion fly), all of which will happily rid your garden of pests.

Ideally, you want to aim for one that increases biodiversity, but your need may be different. For example, according to Kevin Kay of Bessborough Farm, Hernhill, Kent, when first setting up their orchard, it was vital to install a hedge to *filter* the wind not to *break* it. Therefore, they planted *Alnus incana* (grey alder), a member of the birch family and a traditional hedge for fruit growers. When it was established – after the third year – they pruned it accordingly.

To the modern gardener, there is an extensive list of plants available as windbreaks and wind-filters, from trees to grasses – some of the more interesting are included in this chapter. Be sure to understand what the final chosen plant needs and possible problems the plant may acquire over its lifetime. It is unfortunate to point out that in many instances what appears to be

A steel hurdle. An excellent and attractive permanent structure.

A hedge can be anything from a wild and straggly affair to a contrivance of art. The key is to choose the right plant for your needs, your site and your situation. Private residence, Norfolk.

a quick fix in the short-term, often becomes a headache further down the road. A line of trees is a sensible choice if taken wisely, but they do *and will* grow tall if left unchecked. Trees will also remove moisture from the surrounding ground and rob a garden of light if placed anywhere other than to the north. Add to this the unerring habit of gardeners to 'lift' lower branches, the protective screen becomes next to useless, the lower branches no longer furnishing protection. To add insult to injury, a remedial action is to plant a further shelter of shrubs to fill the gap. Beware of this. Once the trees have established, any future planting will struggle, the trees having done their best to remove available nutrients. That said, if you have the space, poplars are a good choice as a windbreak, being utilitarian, sturdy and relatively long-lived.

Ask an Expert

Understanding a plant's physiology is key to understanding gardening. What are the basic methods you use to achieve growing success with new specimens?

Research the plant's natural habitat and environmental conditions. Also look for plants of similar conditions and apply our knowledge of their successful growth. Try to replicate, as best as possible, the natural growing conditions.

Brendan Sayers, Glasshouse Foreman,
National Botanic Garden, Glasnevin, Ireland

Ask an Expert

Is there anything specific you have discovered that is most useful as a protective screen?

We have *Miscanthus sacchariflorus* around some of the container area and it has been a great wind break. It was an accident, as the fence blew down and the nursery was approached about a renewable energy trial in the 1980s, so it got planted. It just can be a bit messy, so makes a job raking it up!

Christine Howard, Managing Director,
Howard Nursery

Something that all husbands of the land must know of is local byelaws. Inconsiderate planting and argumentative neighbours have resulted in laws that limit the height and width of hedges to a certain metreage. If they interfere with neighbouring properties, local councils will enforce measures (including fines) if the problem is deemed a nuisance.

Evergreen Hedges

Following is a short list of recommended evergreen plants. This book has avoided the obvious *'Leylandii'* or *'Thuja'* for the simple fact that whilst they are fast-growing, they offer wildlife very little in either food or shelter and will steal nutrients and moisture from the garden in an adverse way. In the same way, this book does not recommend evergreen *Prunus laurocerasus* or *Buxus sempervirens*, which have increasing problems with pest and disease.

Camelia (*Camelia japonica*)

A glorious hedge, if given the right conditions. It needs an ericaceous soil, so will not tolerate any lime. Prune thoughtfully after flowering to ensure flowers for the following year. Can be host to scale insect and aphids when the young growth is emerging. Once established, it will take quite harsh winters, but any late frost destroys the flower display.

Coprosma repens

Not a fully hardy shrub, this is a plant that needs careful siting as it will not withstand hard frosts. A useful plant in urban areas where frost is rare, or by the coast in the West; it withstands salt spray. It prunes to a neat hedge similar to *Buxus*. Available in a variety of attractive foliage, but be warned – it is named after its unusual smell, so pruning can be interesting. Looser habit than box, it won't hold its shape as well.

Firethorn (*Pyracantha coccinea*)

A neat evergreen hedge can be made of this tough, thorny shrub. Ideal as a security hedge, as only the foolhardy will attempt to push through the vicious thorns. Not expensive to buy, even with quite large specimens. It flowers abundantly given the correct pruning and produces fruits popular with birds. It will

A box hedge parterre with a mulberry at its centre. Garden designers have to wean themselves off the obsession with box. Its downfall is two types of blight and a moth – whose caterpillars will ravage any plant they are lucky to infest. Box has suffered from popularity, the more it is heavily planted in close proximity (see 'Green Bridges', Chapter 7), the worse the problem becomes. Woolly aphid and other pests often overwinter in larger specimens, which causes issues elsewhere. Alternatives are *Coprosma repens*, *Euonymus japonicus* 'Microphyllus', *Santonlina chamaecyparissus* 'Nana', *Taxus baccata* and *Teucrium* × *lucidrys*. Private residence, Kent.

An excellent dividing hedge, camellia provides a welcome and spectacular burst of colour early/late (depending on species) in the year, as well as evergreen screening. Rhododendron could also be used. Private residence.

take quite poor soils, but prefers free drainage. Pruning is painful unless thick 'gauntlet' gloves and shoes are worn! It can suffer from fungal attack.

Kapuka (*Griselinia littoralis*)

Variegation available. An excellent hedge for all situations, including the coast. Fairly slow to grow, the leaves are generally a lush green. It can take a while to establish but is a hardy shrub that is attractive in most settings. A single plant will grow into an attractive tree. It can be bitten by frost, making the leaves scorched in appearance.

Holly (*Ilex aquifolium*)

Variegation available. Holly has many merits, the main being it is evergreen and very tough. It is a slow grower and will take shade, but is expensive to buy as a large specimen. Excellent in a mixed hedge. It has few diseases, excepting a leaf-mining insect that blisters the leaves.

The holly hedge at Kew is often overlooked but is a vital skirt around the palmhouse.

Spindle Tree (*Euonymus japonicus*)

Variegation available. This plant is tough, indifferent to soil and can withstand the harshest of conditions, including the exposed coast. Can be slow to establish and not cheap to buy larger specimens. It can be a harbourage for pests in winter, such as woolly aphid. Suffers from white fly infestations, which can cause leaf fall.

Strawberry Tree (*Arbutus unedo*)

An excellent, low-growing tree with red bark. An unusual, but worthy, evergreen hedge with the added bonus of attractive flowers and edible fruit. It will take a decent pruning if trained early enough. Can suffer from fungal leaf spot, which leads to leaf loss – this problem can be mitigated with a mulch and regular watering/feeding.

Yew (*Taxus baccata*)

Yew is a beautiful hedge and not as slow to grow as some describe. Cheap to buy large specimens, it will take shade well. It has a few downfalls: *Phytophthora* fungal disease is taking its toll (*see* Chapter 8). Rabbits and deer both enjoy eating its young growth.

Euonymus hedge (with holm oak trees above) at Northdown Park, Margate. It provides an excellent shelterbelt for ornamental planting behind that would otherwise be destroyed by harsh winter winds.

BELOW: Yew hedging at Walmer Castle, Kent. It is exceptionally robust and long lived, though fungus can be a danger.

Deciduous Hedges

Following is a list of recommended deciduous plants. As with above, the list is limited to the experience of the author. It is always advisable to see what grows well in your neighbourhood.

NB Most deciduous hedges do not do well in shade.

Beech (*Fagus sylvatica*)

Beech is quite often the 'go to' hedge for many gardens. Available forms are green, purple and bronze. It is quick to establish and keeps its leaves through winter (though not evergreen). It can be pleached, which is an advantage in some gardens where height is an issue or the design specifies vistas. It will tolerate some shade. The downsides are that it does not like to sit in wet, heavy soils and it prefers a high lime content. It will take a fair amount of abuse, but site and soil are its downfall. It can be susceptible to fungal disease.

A deciduous hawthorn hedge in Hood Green, South Yorkshire that has been 'layed' for added strength. Though time-consuming, a layed hedge will create an impenetrable barrier and last much longer than those mechanically flayed. (Layed is the traditional term for a hedge where the stems have been cut halfway through and 'layed' to create a sturdy barrier.)

Birch (*Betula pendula*)

One rarely sees birch as a hedge, but it is a favourite in Northern Scotland as it filters the wind, rather than presenting a solid barrier. It will take being planted close together well. Pruning it into a loose hedge makes the tree produce thicker growth. An excellent idea for more exposed gardens that don't need total privacy. A native of the British Isles, it has few diseases, though pests include a moth and a sawfly, which will strip the leaves.

Forsythia × intermedia

An oft overlooked hedge used in some stately gardens, it will shine in spring when it flowers. It prunes well, creating a decent barrier and is deer and rabbit resistant. Mixed with *Ribes sanguineum* or *Ilex* it makes a stunning display. Needs to be pruned directly after flowering for best effect.

Gooseberry (*Ribes uva-crispa*)

An attractive, low-growing thorny hedge, ideal to break up a garden into sections or around a vegetable garden, with the added bonus of fruit. Grows to 1.5m (5ft) and is suitable for trimming into neat lines. Can suffer from sawfly attack, which strips the leaves.

Hawthorn (*Crataegus monogyna*)

Hawthorn is the cheapest hedge alongside the blackthorn. An indigenous plant, it is a utilitarian hedge. Thorny, it is quite attractive as it flowers well and produces an abundance of red 'haws' in autumn. A good, natural hedge, liked by wildlife, it will take a considerable amount of abuse. It is a favourite food of the ermine moth caterpillar, which can strip a hedge in weeks.

Hornbeam (*Carpinus betulus*)

Hornbeam is a great utilitarian hedge and tree; it grows faster than beech and will take far wetter conditions.

Birch windbreak. An alternative to alder (which is under threat due to climate change and an aggressive fungus). Birch can withstand the harshest of weathers and takes pruning well.

Forsythia spp. is an excellent hedge, much under-used in larger gardens, being relegated to suburban shrubberies, though it is found in some more notable historic gardens. Resistant to both deer and rabbit, mixed with an evergreen, it is a colourful, sturdy and robust alternative to the standard fayre.

Excellent for pleaching. It has a slightly looser habit than beech and does not keep its leaves as well in winter. Leaves can look dusty and jagged if pruned poorly.

Poncirus trifoliata

The trifoliate citrus, a deciduous native of northern China, is an excellent hedge when it can be found. It will take reasonably low temperatures, but not for the more exposed northern gardens. It has formidable thorns that provide an unassailable barrier to almost anything (highly student-proof according to Oklahoma University). A considerably underused option.

Sea Buckthorn (*Hippophae rhamnoides*)

A hedge for a beach. It will take the poorest of soils and the worst weather the sea can throw at it (needs some humus to get going but once established is happy). It produces masses of orange berries high in vitamin C amongst vicious thorns and also traps nitrogen in the soil, aiding other planting. A good alternative is *Tamarix*. Its downside is that it isn't evergreen, meaning that your garden will be a little more exposed in the winter. It also suckers freely, creating a thicket.

Mixed Deciduous Hedges

Very common in gardens, but are also often associated with the boundaries of field systems. These ancient structures are made up of a mixture of species and are excellent for biodiversity. Excellent as a boundary to a larger garden. Generally planted as whips (30cm high), common species are hawthorn, blackthorn, dog rose, Japanese rose, spindle-berry, bullace/mirabelle, oak, ash, hazel, dogwood, holly, field maple and hornbeam/beech (all of which can be used individually or in any combination). The mix depends entirely on taste and situation. It is firmly encouraged that elm species be added – Dutch elm disease only being in evidence in larger trees rather than hedges.

Installing a Hedge

Depending on the space and type of hedge you are intending to install, it is not difficult to install a hedge of reasonable thickness. If you have opted for whips, then it is a good idea to plant a double row in an offset pattern at a thickness of five per metre squared.

If the plant specimens to be planted are larger in size, it is up to the gardener to decide the thickness and numbers needed. If in doubt, ask the supplier who will normally have an idea if you give them the metre specifications, including single or double row. Again, the hole will be different depending on the size and type of plant being used – a whip or bare-root plant will require different husbandry to a root-balled or pot-grown plant.

As a first step, remove all existing plant material (including grass) from the area to be planted (established grasses will compete in the first years of the hedges' growth). Once the strip of land has been prepared, then a trench should be dug.

The mixed hedge is not simply a vital component of farmland. In a garden setting, it provides year-round cover and food for wildlife, encouraging biodiversity. It is also not averse to tight pruning.

Ask an Expert

Why use a native mixed hedge?

Historically, blackthorn was used a lot, and can be seen as a dominant component of many older hedge-lines, creating dense thickets. However, it's suckering/spreading habit makes it less popular among farmers and gardeners alike, especially with the advent of stock fencing.

Nowadays, most providers of hedging will offer a standard 'native mix' or 'wildlife mix', which will normally include 50 per cent hawthorn and then the other 50 per cent will be an even mix of dog rose, field maple, bird cherry, elder – maybe some crab apple or oak. However, it's not clear where this mix, dominated by hawthorn, came from. But it seems hawthorn has taken over as the favourite, providing the spikey-ness of the blackthorn without the suckering nature.

In terms of recommendations for the best mixed/wildlife friendly hedge, I think the answer is a little more nuanced than a simple list with suggested percentages. I would look at the local landscape, look at what grows well, what species in existing mixed hedge-lines are thriving. The soil condition will suit different species. Trees thriving in the Sussex Weald clay will be very different from those on the Dorset chalk downs, Cornish granite rock walls or Welsh uplands.

Lists could be developed for different soil conditions and further refined depending on what part of the country you are in. Coastal areas would benefit from sea buckthorn in the mix, while hornbeam does well in the Sussex Weald clay.

Ultimately, a mix of five or six species should be enough for a mixed native hedge, allowing for further diversification of the hedge through natural colonization. I wouldn't go for 50 per cent hawthorn as standard, but keep the mix more even, so one species doesn't dominate from the off. I would plant the species in blocks of five trees per metre, so again you don't have a single species take over the entire length. For a rule of thumb, look to what is native and growing well locally, and then make sure to include something that will flower for the pollinators, and will then develop fruit (e.g. elder, hawthorn, dog rose, etc.).

Rory Harding, Farmer Cluster Officer,
Kent Wildlife Trust

Things to remember when planting a hedge:

- A hedge planted too deep will struggle and even die.
- The subsoil is often poor in nutrients and should not be used when back-filling any planting hole.
- Soil microbes are vitally important for creating a balanced local ecosystem, so if you are using any compost, mix it well with the existing soil first.
- Put any solid feed into the bottom of the hole to encourage the roots to travel downwards.
- Always water in heavily (even if it is raining). Continue to do this twice a week for several weeks afterwards.
- Always make sure you are planting at the correct time. Changes in weather patterns are increasingly restricting planting times to a slot between late November and early February.
- Do not use a drip feed as a surface pipe. This will encourage surface roots, which do not help the plant establish.

CHAPTER 2

STRUCTURES AND TUNNELS

'Think well all round the subject, and weigh up the pros and cons before you embark on gardening under glass of any kind. Frames and greenhouses are very exacting. You cannot go away and leave them unattended for a week at a time – nor even a weekend – without danger of losing several months' work in a single night or day... There is no New Year under glass – that is to say, there is no beginning to the season, since every month brings rest to some plants and maturity to others'

Richard Sudell,
Secrets of Successful Gardening (1933)

Ask an Expert

Are there any tips you can offer the gardener first thinking of installing a greenhouse?

Greenhouses make an attractive focal point in your garden and instead of being tucked away in a corner, the more elaborate greenhouses are being used as the first point of garden design. The greenhouse provides an attractive environment to grow plants and vegetables all year round, whilst being protected from the elements.

Caroline Griffin, Manager, Kent Sectional Buildings

The next step is to decide if you want to explore further protective measures, such as a fruit cage or greenhouse. Keep in mind what usage the structure will get, what your aims are and how the design will help you to achieve those aims. Once you have assessed your needs, you need to address what is practical, given your space and situation. Remember: something that looks attractive on the eye, may not be very practical.

When buying a protective growing space, use the following questions to assess your needs and the usefulness of the structure:

- Is it within my budget?
- Does it meet *all* my needs?
- Does *form* follow *function*?
- How long will it last?
- Is it easily cleaned?
- Will it withstand the worst of the weather?
- Is it easily repairable or widely recycled?

Fruit Cage

As the name suggests, a fruit cage is built and designed to protect fruit from pest attack – generally birds, but sometimes squirrels and rabbits. The gauge of the net-

The commercial fruit-grower is not only sheltering their crop from the wind but also birds. In crops such as strawberry, the idea is for high yield but low reuse, so all the plants are composted at the end of the season. In fruits such as cherry, the trees are protected from early spring until the last fruit is picked.

Allotments are excellent sources for inspiration when it comes to protecting your crops. Though aesthetics are not the primary concern, they show a high level of imagination and ingenuity.

A fruit cage is not a difficult structure to build if you understand the strengths of the structure and its limitations. This one, at Doddington Place, Kent, is built from steel bars, locked together to form a solid structure. The netting can be removed but the shape is designed to prevent damage from snow.

ting covering the structure will determine what can get inside the growing space. Commercial growers use various frames from square to round.

Some gardeners go to great lengths to build fruit cages to withstand all weathers; depending on the gardener's needs, it need not be a permanent structure at all. For low-growing fruit, such a strawberries or small shrubs, a system of pegged hoops – covered in netting or sheet – can suffice. This can be removed once the season has finished.

Always be aware of weather. Snow will sit on any structure and add considerable weight to it, potentially causing tears or even collapse.

Ask an Expert

Many of the greenhouses one sees today are metal structures. What are the advantages of using wood?

Timber is aesthetically pleasing. Sustainable western red cedarwood has natural anti-rot properties in the way of natural oils. It retains the heat, repels insects, protecting plants and timber alike.

Caroline Griffin, Manager,
Kent Sectional Buildings

Greenhouse

You will come across many shapes and styles of greenhouse, some tried and tested over generations of growers, others mainly the result of a designer's aesthetic whim. All have merit. One factor that is often overlooked and is perhaps the most important of all: What is to be achieved?

Key benefits:

- Sturdy and solid, will withstand most weather conditions.
- Good ventilation included in design.
- Various shapes and sizes to suit your needs.
- Adds architectural interest to the garden.

Key downsides:

- Difficult to move once installed.
- Glass can be difficult to source, especially on unusual designs.
- Can be difficult to clean if very high or odd-shaped.

Wood vs Metal

When first choosing a greenhouse, you will find there is a definite divide between those who like wooden frames and those who prefer metal-framed greenhouses. The majority of greenhouses you will come across will be aluminium. That's not to say that wood is uncommon. Certainly, there are still exceptional manufacturers utilizing wood as the primary material. Indeed, if you were then to use the clear 'glass' made from wood, developed by Lars Berglund at the KTH Royal Institute of Technology (rather than glass made from silicates), one could create an entire structure from wood that lets in 85 per cent of available light with the added bonus of being a natural shade from harsh UV.

Metal has its advantages too. Usually cheaper than wood, it is strong and tolerant of adverse weather – if treated well and cleaned regularly. However, when considering metal, do not assume quality has parity across the cost range. Due to poor manufacturing methods in some foundries, it is important to always make sure you use a certified supplier, that the metal is of good quality and that the guarantee is sound for the expected life of the greenhouse.

NB Aluminium expands and contracts in hot or cold weather, glass will become loose or break due to this action, if not properly built.

Glass vs Plastic Glazing

The main consideration with any structure is allowing the maximum of light to penetrate with the minimum of difficulty. In your journey of protective growing, you will come across a variety of manufacturing techniques from a thin metal frame with cheap plastic covering to a double-glazed, fully automated crystal palace. The first rule is usefulness. The second is sustainability. The third is buy the best you can afford.

The recent abundance of the plastic variety has seen a flush of the small, easy to use, loosely covered plastic sheeting 'greenhouses'. Whilst undoubtedly

Ask an Expert

When building a greenhouse, what are the main considerations?

You may know exactly where you want to site your greenhouse, or you may be seeking advice on which spot will provide you with the ideal temperatures and sun exposure. Many factors contribute to building your greenhouse in the ideal location:

- Consider what you want to grow, and how much light and heat is required to create the right environment.
- Think about how much you want to be able to grow and what size your site can accommodate.
- Observe the site relative to the position of the sun's path from east to west.
- Consider the proximity of large trees around the site.
- Survey the soil and levelness of the ground to see if it is suitable to accommodate the building works and foundations for your greenhouse.
- Look at the surroundings of the site; see if it has enough shelter to protect against prevailing winds and frost.
- Factor in how far the greenhouse would be from your house and how often you would be popping to and from to harvest vegetables and herbs to use in your kitchen.
- Examine the possibility of getting power and water to the structure, for heating and lighting your greenhouse during the darker and colder seasons.

Kitty Yarrow, Alitex

cheap and suited to small spaces, they offer the most basic of protections for the plants inside and are best used as a space much like a cold-frame to harden off plants before putting them out into the garden proper. Admittedly, many have had success growing tomatoes and cucumbers in the limited space, but their design also offers an excellent sweaty environment for pest and disease. How easy are they to scrub clean? They are also incredibly lightweight – being more likely to blow away or to be crushed in winter.

Glass is by far the most versatile of materials, being sturdy, clear, scratch-resistant, relatively insulated, easily washed and easily replaced. Traditionally, greenhouse glass was as thin as possible (about 3mm) to allow as much light as possible to enter, the RHS stating:

> The best glazing material is glass, as it lets 90 per cent of light through, does not degrade in sunlight and, unlike plastic materials, reflects heat radiated from within the glasshouse back into the structure instead of being lost.

Be aware, unless you are restoring a listed greenhouse, when installing glass, modern safety laws means that one has to use 'safety glass', which is the same thickness but considerably stronger.

A Greenhouse Needs Protection

I mentioned in Chapter 1 about protective screens for the wider garden. Practicality is always the primary concern. In turn a greenhouse needs protection from buffeting winds to keep temperatures even and to prevent damage if the weather turns particularly inclement. However, to prevent shading, any useful protective structure should be no less than 5m away, unless on the north side where the sun will struggle to have an effect.

Shapes and Styles

Whether your aesthetic need is for a wood or a metal structure, there are common styles that need careful consideration to suit the space you have available. That said, do not go for what appeals if it is impractical, proves too small or is beyond your physical capabilities to maintain.

Span Roof

This is the 'traditional' shape of greenhouse, with a roof having two equal sides. Ideally, a span roof should be wide enough to accommodate a central staging area, as well as the two narrow side growing areas – however, this is often impractical in modern gardens where space is limited. To some, this form of greenhouse is aesthetically wasteful as it provides the gardener with limited space for display. However, used

The typical span roof greenhouse, though this example is made of wood, many are aluminium. An ideal space for the beginner, it offers the most opportunity to experiment. Goodnestone Park.

correctly, and not forgetting that the central space gives height, which aids heat distribution (*see* Chapter 5), this is by the far the most versatile and, therefore, most common type found, coming in many sizes. As this is a free-standing structure, the building should be placed in a way that utilizes the most light – especially the south and west (*see* Chapter 4 for more detail). The span-roof greenhouse has the positive advantage of being placed in any position the gardener chooses, be it in line of sight or tucked away in a separate area.

Ask an Expert

What size structure would you recommend for the beginner?

8' × 6' (2.4 × 1.8m) is the typical beginner's size, giving a good scope for a good range of general greenhouse gardening. You could maximize that space by adding shelving and staging.

Caroline Griffin, Manager,
Kent Sectional Buildings

Lean-To

The lean-to structure is an incredibly useful design, if you have an existing wall or are intending on building one. It is a building that takes one slope only from back to front. It works best if built facing directly south, but does accommodate any compass-bearing up to due west. If you are growing ferns, a lean-to should face north and is ideal for such purposes. The internal arrangement should be primarily a low, thin stage at the front, a path in the middle and then a stepped stage at the rear wall, so that all the plants receive equal light – but this is down to the purpose and intent of the gardener.

An alternative is to use the lean-to as a house for delicate fruits, such as nectarines and apricots, which flower early and do not appreciate the bite of frosts or rain on their leaves.

The Italianate lean-to greenhouse at King George VI Memorial Park in Ramsgate shows the concept well.

BELOW LEFT: The interior of the lean-to glasshouse at Walmer Castle. The sectioning and internal doors can be clearly seen. By clever use of heating and insulation, this provides a gardener the opportunity to utilize the space for various types of husbandry from succulents to sub-tropical.

Hip Span/Three-Quarter Span

Similar to the lean-to, a hip span is ideal if the wall is too low to accommodate a lean-to. As the name implies, the roof is a combination of the full span and the lean-to, the short 'hip' adding useful height that can accommodate important ventilation.

Dutch/Venlo

Seen as the 'professional' shape, the Dutch greenhouse is engineered to maximize light. Designed specifically to work best in a coastal temperate climate with a high incidence of cloud cover, the span of the roof is exactly the same as the full span greenhouse; where it differs, is the sides. Built at an angle, they maximize the effect of the sun on the crops inside.

Building a Greenhouse from a Manufacturer

If you are lucky enough to have the budget for a brand-new greenhouse, it is always worth buying from a recognized manufacturer. Depending on what shape and style you go for, there will be certain requirements that need to be met before the installation can be completed. These are: adequate siting and adequate footings. The illustrations provide a visual explanation for your reference.

The exterior of the hip span glasshouse at the Farringford Estate, Isle of Wight. The advantage of such a roof is the added ventilation with the protection of the wall. This design is ideal if you are intending on growing fruit trees as well as other plants.

A Dutch or venlo greenhouse. Private garden.

An alternative Dutch style with the side panels at a wider angle to the ground. Private garden.

Following the architectural plans provided, carefully mark out the area making sure it is level, the angles are accurate and the size correct to the millimetre. Once you are satisfied, dig out a trench to the required depth and lay the foundations. Be sure to undertake the correct procedure when building the footings, making sure that the subsoil is of equal firmness and consistency across the entire build. (To prevent 'heave', any soil that is soft or of a different type will need to be dug out until you are satisfied it is capable of sustaining the structure equally.)

Once the concrete foundations are fully set, begin to build the initial structure making sure to check levels and size with the plans as you go. Any mistakes now will cost you time and money later.

The brickwork is complete. Go over the plans carefully with the installer of the glass structure (ideally with the manufacturer) to rectify any snags with things like incorrect angles, levels, etc.).

The completed greenhouse as described, with glass carefully installed under the manufacturer's instruction.

Be Aware!

Working with glass can be hazardous. Take the greatest of care when handling it, making sure all safety precautions have been taken.

Obviously the illustrations are for a greenhouse with a brick supporting wall. If you are installing a type that does not require brick, the same careful approach of checking as you go along is required.

The Commercial House

There is not much difference between a domestic setup and a commercial one – the primary idea of a commercial greenhouse or polytunnel is to maximize space and output, whilst maintaining health and hygiene. To improve growing conditions or if there is a need for growth through the 'cold' seasons, machinery is installed – such as artificial intelligence for plant health, lighting rigs, watering systems, robotic pest control and heat sources.

Polytunnel

The concept of the polytunnel arose in the 1940s. Extremely simple structures, they consist of hooped supports with a covering of protective material. Utilizing the relatively new invention of plastic polythene, they were used in the commercial sector and proved extremely useful in the raising of rain-sensitive crops, such as raspberry or strawberry. This use has since been extended by the use of plastic netting rather than polythene to protect crops – such as cherry – from birds or, as in Italy, to prevent frost damage on citrus.

The role of the commercial glasshouse is mass production. Therefore, health and hygiene are primary concerns. The plants are kept moist via capillary matting or directly via drip.

One of the polytunnels at the Oasis Farm Waterloo, Lambeth. Run on sustainable management techniques, the farm endeavours to be as self-sufficient as possible.

In the domestic and small-holding settings, polytunnels have gained favour with gardeners who want versatility rather than a fixed structure. Being much cheaper than a greenhouse, the structure offers a great alternative. If constructed well, they offer the garden excellent shelter from the wind and rain. There are several manufacturers, all of which should provide you with adequate instruction for this two-person job, in order to construct them properly.

Key benefits include:

- Quick and easy to erect and disassemble.
- Can be moved or be extended (if designed to do so).
- The protective covering can be exchanged for netting or, double layered/have different levels of UV protection.
- Cheaper than glazed greenhouse.
- Easy to clean and easily repaired.
- A number of accessories can easily be purchased.

Some downsides are:

- Condensation build-up if used incorrectly. It is better to buy a polytunnel with a door at either end to create airflow (also install hanging fans).
- Lower light levels. This can be rectified using electricity if needed.
- The metal hoops can heat up causing damage to the polythene. A tape can be purchased to prevent this happening without reducing the overall viability of the space.
- Polythene has a shorter lifespan than glass or other solid plastics.
- A polytunnel can be damaged by careless use of tools. The nature of the plastic means that careless strimming outside, or, indeed, an errant fork or secateurs, can puncture the fabric (metal skirt protectors can be purchased if this is an issue).

Getting the Best from the Polytunnel

Once you are satisfied that the polytunnel is structurally sound, you can start using the space in much the same way as you would a cool greenhouse. As the fabrication is built directly over the soil you intend to use, first look at your growing area. Assess its best use, what can you grow in your soil and situation, taking note that you may have a higher central space than at the sides – a common mistake (though not disastrous) is to create a central path, losing the most creative space in the process. Once you have worked out your planting plan, assess the need for irrigation and where best to place it, so that it reaches the most soil, using the shortest route.

The Polytunnel/ Greenhouse Hybrid

The Polycrub is one of a few hybrid structures that are on the market. Developed and built in the Shetland Islands, UK, it is designed with two purposes: to be fully sustainable in its manufacture – utilizing waste materials from the aquaculture industry – and to withstand high winds and harsh climate, so that food can be grown all year round. Drew Ratter, the Chairman of Nortenergy explains:

> We have supplied Polycrubs to sites very close to the Butt of Lewis, which is officially the windiest place in Britain (though we think Shetland is windier). Before doing that, we commissioned engineering studies on our build, to assess what wind speed could be survived. The results gave us complete confidence, as the ensuing certification gave the Polycrub a survival speed of 120 miles per hour gales. This is well into hurricane force! We now have Polycrubs all over Shetland, all over Lewis and as far afield as the Falkland Islands, and there have been no failures in any crub where the build instructions have been followed. In all or most cases, the far flung Polycrubs are successfully protecting all manner of crops, which would either not be growable or only growable in a narrow window. Hence we now have great confidence in the robustness of the Polycrub, which will stand where no other style of tunnel will.
>
> (Personal correspondence, September 2020)

Cold-Frame

The concept of a cold-frame is simple. If you have limited space, the frame acts as a miniature green house but with a smaller footing. In its traditional form it is a low, square or rectangular shape, higher at the

The Polycrub Classic. An excellent shelter for all weathers.

Cold-frames come in many differing styles, some free-standing as here at Walmer Castle; others are attached to the greenhouse.

back than at the front, with a sloping glass framed top panel that opens upwards. Above all, it should have a brick, concrete or wooden base to conserve heat.

NB Galvanized metal or plastic frames leak heat. In spite of this, the most commonly available are moulded plastic sheeting covering a cheap tubular steel frame – which are lightweight and attractive to the amateur, but should be avoided not only because they are lightweight (thus need anchoring), but because they are short-lived (owing to the weathering effects of the sun) and are incredibly environmentally unfriendly. The cold-frame has four primary uses:

- To harden-off seedlings in spring before being planted out.
- To use within the vegetable garden as a temporary structure to warm the soil before planting or to protect direct sown young crops as they harden off.
- To act as a permanent structure for such plants as early strawberry or winter salads.
- They are excellent to overwinter autumn sown biennials or crops like beans and peas that need protection from heavy winter precipitation.

It is always advisable to think how you want to use your cold-frame. If its primary use is to harden-off crops, then it is an idea to add a mulch of sharp stones to the frame floor to deter slugs and snails, which will enjoy the conditions the space provides. If it is to be used as a growing space, then one needs to look at spatial considerations – understand what you are trying to achieve before experimenting with crops that may outgrow the space. It is outside the remit of this book to explore what can be grown, suffice to say it is an enjoyable past-time to explore the concept of hotbeds or other forcing methods using cold-frames.

Light/Cloche

As with the cold-frame, a cloche is a basic concept having been used in gardens since the fifteenth century. As with other forms of protective growing, the cloche provides individual plants, or perhaps rows of plants, with a protection from frost, wind, birds or flying pests – their most useful trait being that they are entirely portable. There are two main types to consider: the singular form (most often described as a bell, although a variety of shapes can be found, including plastic drinks bottles) and the tunnel form. Most modern cloches are plastic, but glass is still available to the cognoscenti. The positives to using cloches are many:

- Warming the soil to encourage early germination.
- Protection from frosts, heavy rain and pests.

Bell cloches at Bishop's Park, Fulham. They can be a variety of shapes, including upturned plastic bottles and simple low tunnels. The ceramic pots are forcing pots for rhubarb.

- Blanching of certain crops (using black polythene to remove light).
- Overwintering or ripening of certain vegetables.

There are downsides too. Ventilation can be a problem – especially in the single, unopened varieties, which encourages moulds and fungi to prosper. Watering is an issue, unless you introduce a soil-fed watering system before installing the cloche. If you are trying to prevent pest species from having access to the plant, it is highly likely you are preventing access for beneficial insects also – which will lead to irregular pollination. The final issue with the cloche is the encouragement of weed species to flourish.

KG NETT

CHAPTER 3

CULTIVATION AND SOIL

'Everything is joined up, from a single pond to a whole tropical rainforest...We tend to think we are somehow outside of that system. But we are part of it; and totally reliant upon on it'.

Dr Kathy Willis, Professor of Biodiversity at the University of Oxford, *Extinction: The Facts*, BBC Television

Growing Successfully

Above everything else, it is vital that plants get the macro- and micronutrients they need, when they need them. Ultimately, what a plant wants is to grow into a healthy, mature specimen, so that it can pass its genes on to the next generation.

At the most basic level, a plant needs: oxygen, hydrogen and carbon. These it mostly acquires from the air and water (H_2O and CO_2). These three elements are the basic building blocks of 99.99 per cent of all living things on Earth. From the soil or growing medium, a plant requires various macro-elements:

- Nitrogen (N) for growth.
- Phosphorus (P) for roots.
- Potassium (K) for fruit and flower production.
- Calcium (Ca) to aid the transport of substances around the system.
- Magnesium (Mg) is vitally important in the production of chlorophyll.

There are also other elements that a plant requires, which are:

- Sulphur (S).
- Boron gas (B).
- Chlorine (Cl).
- Copper (Cu).
- Iron (Fe).
- Manganese (Mn).
- Molybdenum gas (Mo).
- Zinc (Zn).

These additional micro-elements are needed in smaller quantities to help the plant with some of the more complex chemical processes, such as photosynthesis, or in the production of enzymes and amino acids. All these things can be found in a 'healthy' soil or in the liquid-growing medium that the gardener provides. However, as with everything, they are easily and quickly spent through the growing season and need replacing. Therefore, it is worth remembering the six 'limiting factors' that are necessary for good growth:

1. Water.
2. Air.

Ask an Expert

What is the importance of getting the conditions right?

There are so many variables for different plant types. Understanding the differing plant requirements cannot be over-emphasized. We have a large number of glasshouses and each one has its own separate microclimate that is adapted specifically to grow a particular class of plants: succulents, cacti, ferns, palms, perennials, aroids or sub-tropical leafy plants. Low-tech solutions like orientation to the sun, making use of ambient light or shadow, netting, cool-glass washes, benches and staging, together with insulation and winter fleecing, can all be used to create specific microclimates under glass. Beyond these, ventilation and irrigation are the two most important factors. Using these simple techniques, it is possible to create a wide range of low-cost interior conditions.

John Edmiston, Director of Tropical Britain

3. Food.
4. Enough space to provide good root.
5. It must be at a proper temperature.
6. It must be free from pests, disease or other material likely to be injurious to plant health.

All the factors listed work in tandem and cannot be replaced by another. If the plant is suffering from disease, one cannot simply feed it and expect it to recover. Therefore, a proper supply of the necessary constituent parts is imperative for correct growth. For example, on sandy soil, the limiting factor is both a lack of moisture and a lack of nutrients – therefore, if more water and nutrients get into the soil, the plants will thrive. A cold and wet summer often inhibits plant growth – had the days and nights been a few degrees warmer, the plants would have achieved a better growth.

The Food Web

The food web, as first described by Charles Elton in 1927, describes the interconnected processes in which all life relates to other species, genera and kingdoms. This cycle involves a producer, primary consumer, secondary consumer, tertiary consumer, final consumer and decomposer – a simple concept that has complex implications. Traditionally, we are taught that at the most basic stage, the soil and the photosynthesizers therein, are the 'primary level' – there being many levels above, with humans at the apex. However, with biodiversity in critical decline across the planet, it is obligatory that any gardener understands the wider scope of what he, she or they are trying to achieve, and that this primary level is far more complex than simply providing food.

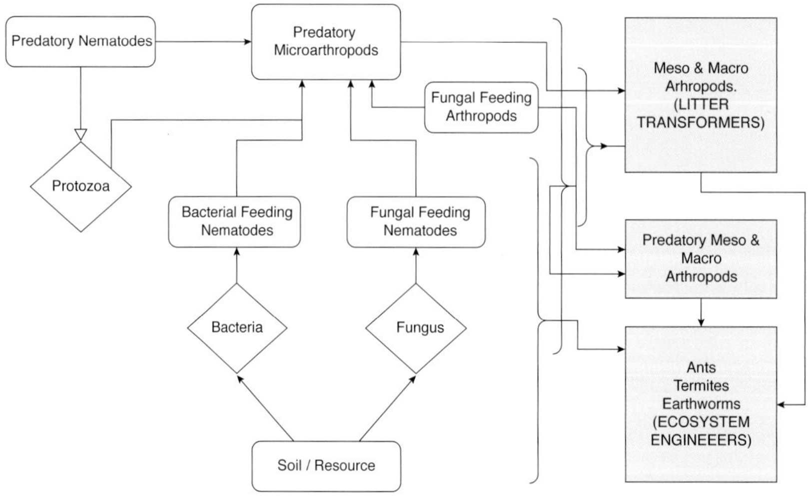

The soil food-web is a complex and intricate interdependency. Based on information from Coleman (2011).

At a microscopic level (and at its least understood), microbes and fungi in the soil are the 'decomposers' and 'releasers/producers'. Plants, earthworms and other small invertebrates will feed on these released nutrients. These basic forms of life live in an almost symbiotic and vital relationship, each having great importance to all other life cycles. The microbes break down minerals into soluble materials that the plants and invertebrates can absorb. The plants return the favour, by releasing sugars that the microbes and fungi feed on – some plants will actively supply nutrients to its plant neighbours too. (The plant also plays willing host to beneficial fungi and bacteria, opening the soil and holding it together.)

On a macroscopic level, the plant is seen as the simple 'producer', while the insects that feed on the plant are the primary consumers. These primary consumers, pests though they are, have predators such as birds, mammals or other insects, which are known as secondary consumers and are part of a wider biodiversity. In this way, the chain continues, creating a 'web' of life – all of which returns to the soil and decomposes to start the cycle again.

Without this incredibly delicate balance, the garden rapidly loses its vitality. It must also be understood that the environment does not decay over a linear path – one insignificant element disappearing at a time – in actuality a gradual build-up leads to total collapse across the entire local ecosystem.

Testing the Soil

Before starting any project in your growing space, it is always advisable to get an accurate, professional test done to assess what your garden needs, what it has too much of and what may be detrimental to the plants that you are aiming to grow – an abundance of one chemical can, and does, inhibit the release of other vital chemicals.

There are various agronomist companies (such as FAST) that will test your soil for a fee or, if you are on a budget, testing kits can be bought from a good horticultural supplier.

Getting the balance right is often simple, but it is advisable to seek the knowledge of a professional in the first instance. (Simply adding deficient nutrients can sometimes have disastrous effects and encourage disease.) Be sure to include a pH test in the soil study

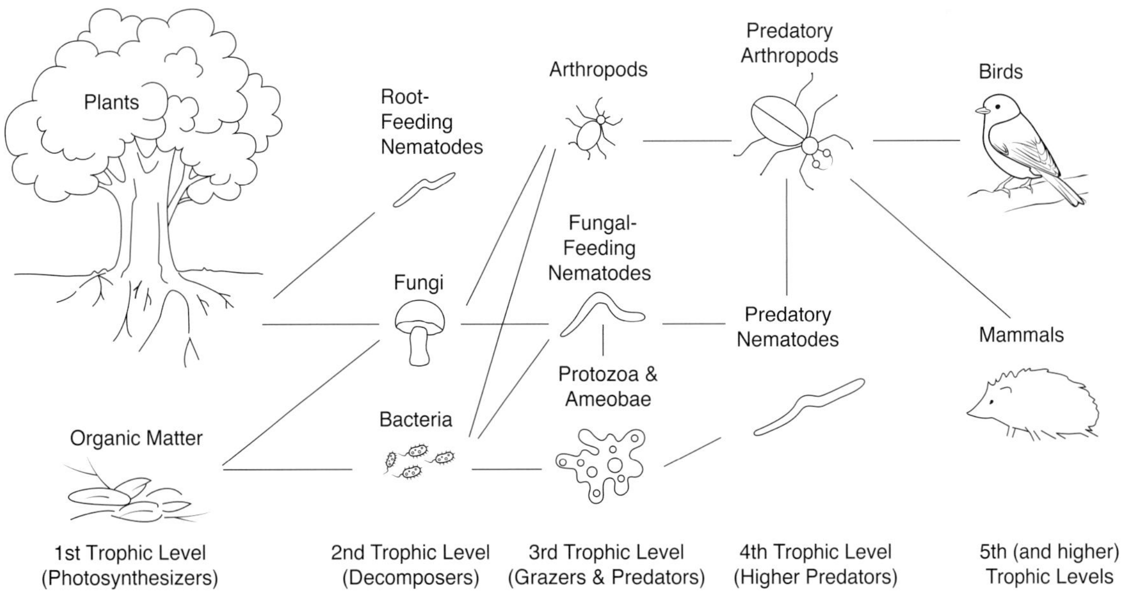

The macro food-web based on USDA information.

An eroded river bank at Swalecliffe, Kent exposes the various soil layers to the elements. The most fertile layer is in the top few centimetres. The thick black layer 30cm down is organic matter deposited when the area was used as a rubbish dump to act as a sea defence. Below this is yellow brick clay, grey 'London' clay and other deposits dating back to the Ipswichian, Devensian and Early Holocene. Due to the nature of the area, the soil strata is somewhat mixed. Other areas may be less damaged, but it depends on land usage prior to investigations.

(*see* section on pH). Whilst it may not appear vital, a soil that is either too acid or too alkaline can affect your growing results, permanently locking nutrients into the soil. When this occurs, no manner of adding fertilizer will change the results and you may actually be compounding the issue.

Effects of pH on Soil

The pH represents to chemists the acidity or alkalinity of a solution on a logarithmic scale, where 7 is neutral, 1 is very acid and 14 is very alkaline. Getting the pH right is key to unlocking all the food a plant needs. As with everything, chemical reactions occur with the addition and reduction of any constituent part of the healthy soil. Always assume your actions are somehow affecting the pH balance, by the simple act of digging, watering, adding mulch or introducing fertilizers.

Some fertilizers have an acid effect, others an alkaline effect. As these introductions into the closed environment of a greenhouse or polytunnel do not have the facility to leach out due to rain or weather erosion, they will cause a build-up in the soil, eventually becoming toxic if left unchecked. To some extent, remedial actions can be taken to balance the build-up – the addition of garden lime to de-acidify or humic acid to lower alkalinity. In the long term, fresh soil will have to imported.

Table 1 Fertilizer pH

Gypsum	Neutral
Lime	Alkaline
Sulphur	Acid
Superphosphate	Neutral
Sulphate of ammonia (do not add to clays)	Very acid
Ammonium nitrate	Acid
Potassium sulphate	Neutral
Urea	Slight acid

Types of Soil

Soil is formed from the decomposition of rocks, under the influence of rain, sun, frost, air and living organisms, such as lichens. The finer the decomposition, the more readily nutrients are available to the plant. Wherever you are and whatever the circumstances it is very rare that any two garden soils are alike. They may have compaction, they may have erosion, salt build-up or have had compost added.

NB It must be noted for clarity that soils without any organic matter (material from decomposed animal or vegetable matter known as humus) are not fertile. For a soil to become fertile, it *must* have an addition of humus.

Ask an Expert

Are there any unusual circumstances you have come across in dealing with soil?

In a garden I dealt with in the Kent Weald, the garden had two types of soil running through it. On one half, the soil was greensand – an extremely porous and fertile growing medium prized as a joy to gardeners. It is acid in nature, so is ideal for ericaceous plants. The other half was heavy marl (a clay that's good for brick-making) with poor drainage and very sour only a few feet down. The major problem with this garden was how to address the immediate issue of soil structure. Both soils have issues with drainage. The sand 'leaches' quickly leaving the soil devoid of nutrients; the clay was locked and compacted. To add just any compost could have been disastrous to the plants if the pH was changed. Careful consideration was taken. After an assessment of the garden needs, it was decided to add a simple soil improver as a mulch – rather than enriched compost. This would not affect the pH, would add structure and aid the microbiome by encouraging worms and other invertebrates. Future mulches would involve the introduction of locally sourced leaf mould, which would aid structure without adversely affecting the overall environment.

G. P. Roland, retired Head Gardener from Kent

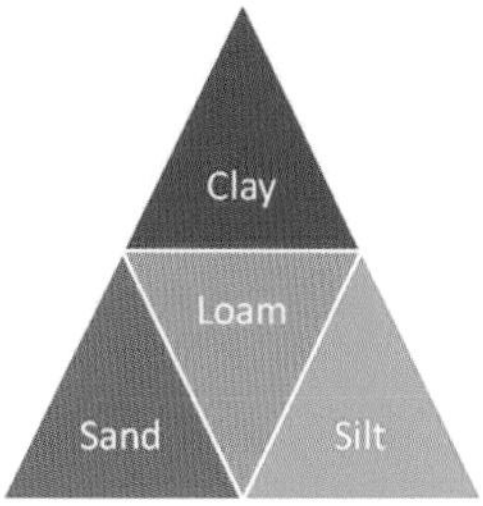

A schematic of the different soil types.

The basic premise of gardening is to assess your soil and to work with what you have. As already alluded to, the four basic soils are: clay, sand, silt and loam. As one would expect, they have their own individual construction and their own individual strengths and weaknesses.

Be aware of your soil health. Important to soil, the St. Mark's fly (*Bibio marci*) is seen as a pest. The larvae spend their time breaking down leaf litter, other organic matter and compost heaps. The adults are important pollinators.

Clay

Daphne Ledward, in her book *The Idiot Gardener's Handbook* (1987), introduces clay in the following way:

> This type of soil is the gardener's horror, which sticks to the boots when wet, and dries out to rock-hard during dry spells in summer.

Surprisingly, to some, clay is incredibly rich in nutrients, holding them well – unfortunately much of it is locked and needs work to be released. Depending on the rock strata below, it can be acid or alkaline. As described by Daphne Ledward, its attributes cause problems for plants that are trying to survive in such an adverse growing medium. Its structure is made up of platelets (that resemble tiny plates) that, when compressed, form a more than adequate barrier to anything. Due to its nature, it is a cold soil throughout winter, warming slowly as the sun acts on it in spring.

Ask an Expert

Keeping the soil healthy is key to good plant health. What approaches should be taken given that you have so many different environments?

At Kew we mulch our beds at least once a year, this brings biological life (microbes, fungi and bacteria) into the soil, as mulch is usually rich in biological life. There are many things that can be used as a mulch, including food waste, grass clippings and other garden waste. If one has a compost heap, the product is perfectly suited. Compost teas are also a good way to improve soil health but that is a big topic!

If fertilizers are used, stick to the manufacturer's recommendations and try to use organic ones; mineral feeds tend to kill off a lot of biological life but can be used sparingly.

Soil also needs to be aerated (can be done with a fork) to improve structure. Compacted soil is usually poor for growing plants, as it has little air, which roots need to grow healthily. Not always easy if one is growing long-lived plants! In this case, mulching and good biological life are important as the microbes, bacteria, worms, etc. will do this for you.

Scott Taylor, Conservatories Manager,
Kew Gardens

Clay is typically made up of particles less than 0.002mm in size. They are in the shape of flat platelets and are easily compressed.

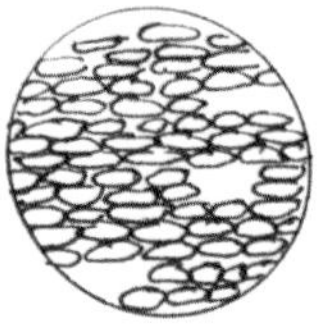

An image of clay (*left*) with an illustration of how the 'platelets' are structured. Do not assume all clays are the same. Lower Wealden clay is remarkably full of silt and is sometimes seen as unworkable.

Sand particles are characterisitcally irregular shaped and are generally between 0.05 and 2mm in size.

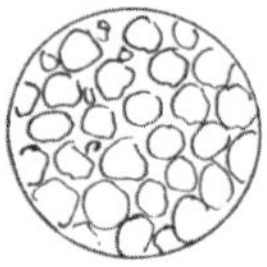

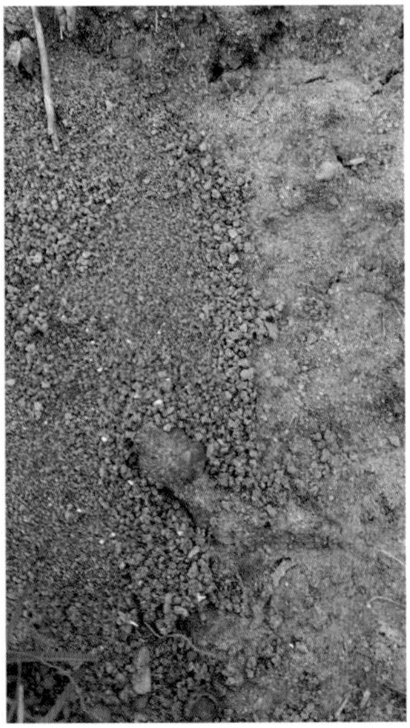

An image of sand (*right*) with an illustration of the larger particle structures.

This can be an advantage – the soil temperatures remaining remarkably stable. Many gardeners looking at the structure of clay are wrong to assume the best answer is to add sand. Add a good mix of well-rotted manure, soil improver and grit at a ratio of 2-3-1. Another way of opening clay is via 'flocculatation'.

Sand

Most often because of its sandstone parentage, the high iron content makes sand acid. It is easy to dig, easy to manage and equally easy to lose nutrients through 'natural leaching'. It also has the annoying habit of forming a surface 'pan' when it dries out,

Silt particles are typically between 0.002 and 0.05 mm. They are not uniformly shaped and include clay platelets.

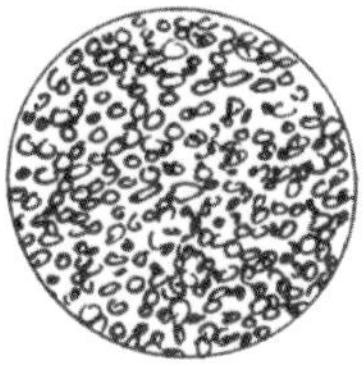

An image of silt with an illustration of how the particles are distributed.

making watering next to useless. Made up of a mixture of small to large particles of rock and silicates, it has a very loose structure. It warms quickly in spring but is easily penetrated by surface frosts to a surprising depth. Add a good mixture of well-rotted farm manure and soil improver at a rate of 1-1.

Silt

Created mainly by water erosion, it is found on alluvial plains or near rivers. Depending on the salts deposited, it can be either acid or alkaline, but the majority is slightly acidic. Made of tiny particles washed downriver and deposited during flooding, it is, like clay, highly nutritious to plants. However, like a clay and sand combination, it can be difficult to manage – turning to a useless slushy soup if over-watered or, if too dry, easily compacted, eroded or 'panned'. Add to the soil a good mix of rotted animal manure and soil improver at a rate of 1-1.

Loam

The ideal soil in any garden is somewhere between all three previously stated types. The perfect mix has been suggested as 50 per cent sand, 30 per cent clay/silt, with natural fibres and compost making up the rest. It is also suggested that it has a high lime or chalk content to further enrich the growing environment. The healthier the soil, the better the micro-biodiversity. Therefore, it is in your best interests to learn what you have and to improve it steadily over time.

Improving Your Soil

It generally takes 500 years for nature to create just two inches of good topsoil, yet archaeological finds show that a great deal more substance is added over that time. This soil is not necessarily good, it having been created by human activity or by wind movement, transported by water and so on – any subsoil at the surface sours land as it is generally infertile. The best way forward, therefore, is to improve your soil by two separate means, which are to manually remove sour or 'spent' soil and to add a suitable improver as outlined in this chapter.

In the case of planting a protective hedge, it is a good idea to dig a trench approximately 70cm in depth, being careful to keep aside the healthy top 50cm and discarding the rest (this calculation is done based on best-case scenario, the soil in your plot may be very shallow before it reaches the poorer subsoil). Then carefully import a 50/50 mixture of well-rotted manure and topsoil, adding it to the trench along with your good, existing topsoil. This process is time-consuming and can be expensive, but gives the plants the best opportunity to thrive. From a practical point of view, many professional gardeners would just recommend digging a slit trench and planting 'as is'. This is the most economic method available and is not without its merits – it works well with young whips – however, it is more reliant on guesswork, the plants having a greater exposure to infection, water-logging or drought.

These processes can be followed in the greenhouse or polytunnel; however, this should only be done to give your growing space the best start. All other imports of fresh compost/soil, as noted in Chapter 7, only require the top 30cm of soil to be replaced. Continue to add compost in small quantities over the year.

Mulching

This technique involves the spreading of a layer of rotted manure, leaf mould or some similar substance over the surface of the soil. The object of the task is twofold: first, to feed the plants and add structure to the soil; second, to act as a 'blanket' for the roots of plants. It is good to note it also has a third use, which is to suppress weeds. Many books describe mulches as most useful in the spring and early summer – but be warned, if it is applied too early in the year, it could inhibit growth as it acts as an insulator for cold soil. If applied too late, as the summer heats up, it will just sit at the surface doing nothing – the worms and invertebrates having been driven too deep to have practical purpose. Therefore, the simplest way is to touch your bare elbow to the soil: if it feels cold, then it is too early to mulch; if the soil looks dry and crumbles in your hand, then it is too late. A mulch in late autumn is always a good addition to your garden calendar, as it gives the soil a chance to restock over its 'fallow' time.

Making Compost

Compost is not merely a matter of throwing any kitchen and garden waste on to a pile and letting the garden fauna 'do their thing'. Certain foods and plant material should never be added, so always consider your actions. Large chunks of wood should be discarded or shredded first. Citrus fruits are too acid for many garden compost heaps or bins, so should be left to steep in water for a few weeks before being added to the heap. Eggs and eggshells will most likely attract the attention of rodents such as rats, which will cause a nuisance, and they also take a considerable time to break down, unless crushed first. Weed species, such as horsetail, dock, creeping buttercup or nettle roots, should never be added to the pile, as you will undoubtedly spread the problems further around your plot.

Manures

Manures come in many different forms and have equally as many characteristics. Many will contain nitrogen, phosphates and potash, but not in the right proportions needed for all plants, so heavy use is on an advisory basis. Analysis varies depending on what the animals have been fed on, bedding used, its age, where it has been stored and so on. If stored well, manures tend to become richer as microbes begin the process of breaking it down. An average breakdown of a well-rotted stable or farmyard manure is as follows:

- Nitrogen 0.5–1 per cent; 4–8kg per tonne.
- Phosphate 0.5 per cent; 4kg per tonne.
- Potash 0.5–1 per cent; 4–8kg per tonne.

Green Manures

An excellent resource. Used properly, green manures can add biomass to the soil, add nutrients and prevent pest infestation, if researched first. The premise is to sow over the area a seed – such as clover or *Phacelia* – allowing the plant to grow but not flower, then digging it into the soil.

NB For this to be successful, the plant must be entirely dug in and the area then left to decompose for a period.

Horse Manure

Though the most common of manures, horse manure is possibly the least useful in the garden on its own. The horse gut is short and has fewer microbes than other herbivores, so invariably weed seeds survive the journey through the alimentary canal. It is far better to add horse manure to your compost heap and allow the vital nutrients to be released by the microbes, whilst the weed seeds are destroyed by the heat. Horse manure is most useful for heavy clay soils, as the constituent parts mark it out as an excellent soil improver.

Cow Manure

A good basic manure. The gut of a cow is more complex than a horse, the cow having a number of stomachs, so it can be readily used as a mulch. It is excellent on lighter soils, adding water-retentive qualities. An average dressing is one barrowful (50kg) to $8m^2$.

Pig Manure

Rich in nitrogen, it is excellent for poor, sandy soils. It should be stacked in the dry for some months before use, as it can contain unpleasant toxins that are harmful to both you and the garden.

Chicken Manure

Very rich in nitrogen, excellent when added to the compost heap as a raw material – never add it to the beds raw, as it will cause issues with your plants. If left undercover for an adequate time to mature (usually a month or two), the average content of NPK is 4-3-1. Alternatively, it can be purchased already treated in buckets as handy granules. Follow the dressing guidelines very carefully to avoid over-feeding.

Urine

Rich in nitrogen and potash. Unusual to find, very useful nevertheless. Night-water, as it was known, used to be a valuable commodity.

Insect Frass

An insect manure created from the exotic pet industry, it is the castings of mealworms or crickets. Contains a basic level of plant nutrient with an average NPK of 2-2-2. It is also touted as a pH balancer. Very useful for indoor growing and for hydroponic users, it boosts plant immune responses.

Seaweed

Seen as a valuable alternative to dung. Rich in potash but lacking in phosphates. A good addition to your compost heap. Be aware, there are laws governing what can be removed from beaches, so check the local byelaws before procuring. Average NPK for fresh seaweed is 0.3-0.1-1.

Compost from Council Dumps

Whilst commercial composting can reach far greater heats than a common garden compost bin, there are pitfalls. Depending on the time of year, there is a risk of higher salt content if the compost was made using winter-collected material. There is also a high chance of plastics being in the mix. Anecdotal evidence has found this to be true on farmland and allotments that use council-contracted composts or soil improver. Notwithstanding, the NPK is generally 0.45-0.5-0.5.

Peat

Restricted from all types of commercially bought compost, peat is technically a type of soil made from centuries of anaerobic decomposition of mosses in an acid bog environment. A highly controversial soil improver, its high carbon storage capabilities and its environmental worth as a unique habitat are now internationally recognized as vitally important to halt climate change. Therefore, due to the destructive methods of extraction, its usage is becoming rare. It is an excellent addition to soils that lack the capability to hold on to moisture or soils that need an external source of structure. Acid in nature, it needs to be balanced unless you are aiming at creating an acid garden, as at Bressingham in Norfolk. Coir (coconut husk), shredded wool and shredded bracken are often used as viable alternatives.

Fertilizers

Blood

An excellent source of immediate nitrogen. Dried blood should be used at a rate of 30g per square metre. Wear a mask when handling. NPK rate is generally 8-0-0.

Blood, Fish and Bone

A common fertilizer available across a range of retail outlets. Average NPK rate is 4-7-4. It is a decent all-round fertilizer, encouraging strong root growth, building soil fertility, aiding growth and fruit and flower production. There is controversy with regard to sustainability.

Bonemeal

Seen as an excellent source of phosphate, it is a by-product of the meat industry. Depending on the coarseness, it can take a long while to break down, risking a reduction in nitrogen. NPK value generally 3-15-0 but it can be as high as 2-22-0. Application rate 100g per square metre.

Chalk

An interesting soil type, it is made up of rounded calcareous platelets derived from dead, ancient, marine animals known as coccoliths. In its natural form it is thin, poor in nutrients, badly drained, with a habit of

A bag of organic fertilizer. Bought from professional suppliers, they are clearly marked with their N, P, K content. It is always important to ask your supplier the constituent parts, as they may be unsuitable for your type of soil, thus testing is vital.

Be Aware!

When dealing with any type of fertilizer, it is important to treat them with respect. Always wear the appropriate clothing and follow the guidelines. For many of the chemicals, you will need to be in the open air or a well-ventilated area, and use gloves (and mask), weighing scales and/or a measuring jug. Always read the instructions closely. Be aware. All fertilizers will add to salt build-up in a closed environment and add to soil stress.

turning to mush when wet. Ground down and dried, it is highly useful on acid or clay, but can both lock in and lock out other nutrients.

Hoof and Horn

A great-acting addition to potting compost at a rate of 1g per 30ltr of John Innes No.3. Add direct to the soil as a top dressing at 50g per square metre. NPK analysis is close to 12-0-2.

Lime

Common garden lime is generally calcium oxide, calcium hydroxide or sometimes calcium carbonate (*see* Chalk). Lime is added to the soil as a 'sweetener'. In general terms, the different kinds all act the same – some quicker than others. Lime does have the benefit of changing the soil pH, if this is an issue, but if the nutrient balance is wrong (especially magnesium), you could encourage some destructive slime moulds. Best practice is to be cautious with application at 350g per square metre. Do not confuse with quicklime.

An alternative to garden lime is gypsum (calcium sulphate), which is neutral so will not affect the overall soil pH. It is an excellent agent for improving soil structure, particularly on heavy, waterlogged soils. A dressing of 200g per square metre is usual. Dolomitic limestone is another useful combination of calcium carbonate and magnesium carbonate. Primarily used to neutralize acid soils, it provides additional magnesium if deficient. Best used when a knowledge of the soil is available, at the recommended argronomist's rates.

Liquid General Purpose Plant Food

A catch-all plant food manufactured by countless brands, it is always vital to know your garden needs. NPK values vary massively, depending on what has been created. Miracle Grow™ is 24-8-16, others are 25-25-25 or 8-12-8. Follow the manufacturer's guidelines very carefully.

Liquid Seaweed

Depending on the manufacturer, the qualities of this type of feed have many benefits, including as a foliar feed. Always read the manufacturer's notes on uses, application rates and NPK values – they differ widely. Touted as helping biodiversity, be aware that without the benefit of weathering action, they do add to a build-up of salts.

Liquid Tomato Feeds

Specifically manufactured and aimed at producing an abundance of fruit, the average NPK rate is 4-3-8. Follow the manufacturer's application rates carefully. An alternative is making homemade 'comfrey tea', which has similar properties and is better for the soil overall. (Collect a good amount of comfrey leaves and steep in a bucket just covered by water for several weeks. Strain, putting rotten leaves on the compost heap. Store. Dilute the liquor before use: 1 part comfrey to 10 parts water. Nettles can replace comfrey if none available.)

Nitrate

Not easy to get hold of for the amateur gardener and extremely dangerous if stored or handled inappropriately. It is applied in spring and early summer. Various forms include nitrate of potash (saltpetre) – *do not confuse with potash nitrate* – nitrate of soda and nitrate of lime. All are soluble forms of nitrogen, a rich, quick-acting fertilizer. They have a caustic effect on the leaves of plants if misused. Care should be taken when handling, *do not breathe in*. Read the manufacturer's notes for the rate of application.

Potash Salt

Applied in autumn and winter. Available in various forms. High content of potash, generally between 20 and 30 per cent. Follow specific manufacturer's guidance carefully for rates of application, but generally 30g per square metre.

Sulphate of Ammonia

A nitrogenous fertilizer, much safer than nitrate, as not so quick acting or caustic. Must not be mixed with lime. Rate of application is generally 30g per square metre, but always follow the manufacturer's guidelines.

Superphosphate

The quickest way of applying phosphates. It will not affect the acidity of the soil. Rate of application is 30g per square metre.

Wood Ash

Still readily available if you have a wood-burning stove. A useful, but variable source of potash. The amount present is based on the type, age, method of storage and condition of the wood burned. A good NPK is 15 per cent but more likely to be nearer to 4 per cent in most cases. Apply with conservative application rate of between 100g and 200g per square metre.

Manures and Fertilizers that Must Never be Mixed

Chemistry is a complex and skilled profession and not for the hobbyist. Some substances react violently if mixed with other substances. The most important to remember are lime with raw chicken manure, nitrates with any acid, sulphate of ammonia with chalk or lime. Also, superphosphate must never be mixed with anything containing lime or chalk.

Downsides to Using Imported Manures and Composts

Depending on the size of area you are likely to be utilizing, it will be of benefit to bring in compost. Obviously the best compost is from your own garden. It is estimated that one teaspoon of garden soil will have up to one billion microbes. However, over recent years, an increased incidence of soil poisoning has been reported by organic farmers – most notably from pesticide and fertilizer residues. This obviously has an effect on whatever you are trying to grow, especially if that plant (most likely dicotyledonous) is directly affected by the chemicals in the soil.

Watering

It may appear a counter-intuitive argument to explain watering, but it is one operation that is commonly misunderstood. Obviously, knowing your plants and their requirements is important, but within the context of watering, the depth of soil is key in any operation. In the heat of a greenhouse, a growbag will lose moisture more quickly than a well-prepared bed.

The idea is to water heavily, less often, rather than little and frequently. Therefore, with a growbag, it would be an idea to introduce the 'wick method' (*see* Hydroponics) – this will ensure that the bag has access to a constant moisture source. For an established bed, the idea is that it is has enough water-holding resource, so mulching at least yearly will aid this retention.

Water heavily at times when the sun is not at its hottest, always on the soil, not on the plant. In the case of trees, this means leaving the tap on for a considerable time – especially if you are new to the space and are unsure of when it was last watered properly.

Keep draughts to a minimum, but with good ventilation, so that the water does not evaporate needlessly out of the space. Syringe (keep wet) hard surfaces a few times a day in order to raise the humidity. This will put off pests such as red spider mite and reduce evaporation from the beds.

For hedges, always plant them in late autumn or early winter, so that they have some time to adjust and grow during the fallow months – do not rely on the fabled wet spring months, climate change has altered weather patterns permanently. Water them in heavily and, if they look parched, water them – even in winter and regardless of light rain or showers. (Depending on your soil, it takes many hours of heavy rain to penetrate any soil properly. A saturated soil dries quickly in wind.)

By following a simple system of rules, you should achieve success:

- Check the weather and know the season. Water will evaporate quicker during hot spells than cold.
- Know your plants. Some plants require little water, others require lots – some plants even require a rest period when no water should be given at all. The majority of the time you will be able to tell if a plant is suffering from lack of water by the way the leaf hangs. Wilting *may* be a sign of lack of water.
- Check the soil by pushing your finger in to a depth of 3cm. If it is damp, then there is enough water in the soil. If the plant is still wilting, it may be a sign of root-rot (*see* Chapter 8).
- If the soil is dry, then soak it well, trying to avoid getting any on the plant. Always water well and less often.

When planting a new specimen or hedge, make sure that the root-ball or pot is left to soak first. Once installed, water the surrounding soil heavily, saturating to a depth beyond the existing root. Keep watering if the hedge is competing with local flora.

Water butts and collection tank at the Garden Gate Project, Margate. Utilizing all available water sources is vital and it should be collected at every opportunity.

Mulching to Reduce Watering

If you are intending to leave areas fallow over winter, it is an idea to mulch in late autumn, letting the soil fauna break down the material rather than digging it through. This will aid the microbiology and also improves drainage to a surprising depth in soils such as clays.

Automatic Watering

There are many forms of automatic watering systems that you can use. Depending on your situation, these can vary from a simple timer and sprinkler or drip hose to a fully computerized system. It is not within the remit of this book to discuss the merits of every conceivable method of watering, suffice to say, careful consideration must be taken with regard to your soil, situation, availability of water and water wastage.

Always be aware of the manner in which you are watering. If you aim to use a drip hose, or other irrigation systems, the local water pressure may not allow for the water to flow effectively beyond a certain metreage. If this is the case, you will need to install a pump system in order to increase water pressure. Ask the manufacturer (not the seller) for details on how far their drip-hose will reach effectively. By watering lightly or on the surface, you will be encouraging the roots to only spread across the surface of the soil – this will reduce drought resilience.

Mulching is an incredibly useful tool in the gardener's armoury. Not only does it add soil structure but it helps retain moisture through the growing season. Depending on the type of mulch used, it can be planted through. This illustration is year-old chicken bedding hay being used over early potatoes.

Ask an Expert

How does your drip-hose work and what is the flow rate/pressure requirements and maximum length of hose for optimum use?

Instead of manually watering beds and borders, the Flopro Soaker Hose can be connected to your outdoor hose with or without a timer to automatically water plants. The hose is made of a porous pipe, so the water can seep out at a pressure of 0.5–3bar (7.5–45psi)/leakage: 1–10ltr/m/h. It slowly releases water along its 15m length to assure economical, as well as precise, plant watering, reducing evaporation by an estimated 70 per cent. Place your soaker hose under the surface of the soil at a recommended depth of 15–20cm.This soaker hose has been designed to work at low water-pressure only. Open your tap quarter to half a turn only. The water will start to seep out slowly, which is perfect for getting direct to the roots. If you require a longer length, you can connect another soaker hose. Use a maximum of two soaker hoses together at any one time to enjoy optimum performance. Simply unscrew the end cap from the first hose, unscrew the male end from the second hose and then attach these two ends together to create the connection.

Natalie Searle, Westland Horticulture

Capillary Matting

The concept of capillary matting is simple. Using the 'wick method', the matting absorbs and holds water, keeping a film layer of moisture available for the plants that are placed in their pots on specifically designed staging or trays. The advantage of this method is that the water supply can be kept constant and aids moisture retention in the air of the growing space.

However, there are downsides. The main problem is a tendency for algal growth if hygiene is not maintained (this can be negated by washing the mats with detergent every few months). Depending on your manufacturer, the matting can be made of wool, cotton or polyester.

A commercial 'flood and drain' hydroponics system. Despite its efficient use of water and hygiene potential, hydroponics is still very much seen as solely for professionals, geeks or experimentalists.

Hydroponics – a Useful Alternative?

Hydroponics has a long theoretical history, its use dating back to the later stages of World War II. Given that global warming has already started to affect rain patterns, hydroponics may be an answer to future water-usage issues. Indeed, hydroponics has established itself in many urban agriculture and commercial growing operations. Utilizing a carefully monitored nutrient-rich liquid fed directly to the plant's roots, it uses less water than traditional methods – creating less stress on a limited water resource. It is hygienic (if the liquid is kept clean and replaced before algae builds up), resulting in reduced pesticide use – in theory giving higher productivity in less space.

For the amateur or beginner, it is recommended to follow one of three simpler pathways with which to establish an understanding:

1. The wick method – a very old method of supplying water and/or extra nutrients to the plant via a wick sitting in a reservoir below. (This method is a half-way house between traditional growing and hydroponics, where the plants are still grown in

A manufactured water trough for the domestic market utilizing the wick method. Simple to use, the trough is filled with water and the grow bags are placed carefully over the raised wick points, to allow the soil to remain moist. The downside to this method is that, if not carefully installed, soil contaminates the water reservoir below causing issues with hygiene. This system could be used with liquid nutrient and pumice, which would reduce these issues.

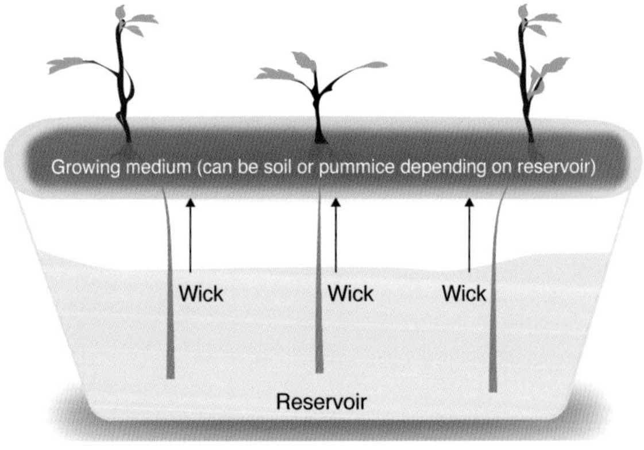

Hand watering can be done using a watering can or hose. The installation of watering systems (as in this commercial grower) is also of benefit, but make sure the system is set up to water according to the rule of watering heavily and less often.

compost bags or the growing medium on top of the reservoir.)

2. Hand-watering. Having first placed the young plants in an inert medium, such as a hay bale, water the plants on a regular basis to provide them with adequate nutrients to thrive.
3. The nutrient film method – a true hydroponic system where the plants grow in a non-reactive medium, such as pumice or coir, and are supplied with nutrients via a flow of liquid. It is advised that a 6ft (1.8m) greenhouse will hygienically accommodate four to five plants along its length.

If you wanted to explore all the options, there are several variations (*see* Table 2). It is best practice to research, before purchase, the system you wish to employ considering these factors: plant growing habit, space, time, budget, ease of use, ease of operation and energy supply.

Table 2 Hydroponics variations

Hand watered	The simplest method. The plants are grown in inert growing materials, such as straw or pumice stone. They are watered with a nutrient solution by can or hose. A remote automatic watering system can be utilized.
Nutrient film	The plants are suspended above the nutrient solution on an angled ramp. A pump continuously bathes the plant roots with the solution, which then returns to the reservoir below.
Drip system	The plants are suspended over a reservoir of nutrient solution on a permeable tray. A pump draws water from the reservoir to the above tray to a drip system. Unspent liquid is returned to the reservoir below.
Flood and drain	The plants are suspended over a reservoir of nutrient solution on a permeable tray. A pump draws water from the reservoir to the above tray on a timer, to flood the tray periodically. Unspent liquid is returned to the reservoir below or discarded elsewhere.
Aquaponics	The plants are placed in a reservoir of water filled with fish. The plants feed on the waste products that the fish produce and filter out the water. Currently used in some experimental heating projects where the fish-spoil and grown plants are utilized in an aerobic digester.
Aeroponics	Developed by NASA to utilize limited resources such as water. The plants are suspended above the nutrient solution reservoir – the roots are misted with an aerosol of the solution.
Deep-water culture (DWC)	Plants are permanently suspended in a nutrient-rich solution. Air is pumped into the solution to prevent the plant from drowning.
Top-fed DWC	As in normal DWC, the plants are permanently suspended in a nutrient-rich solution and aerated. The difference is that the plants are in a container and are also fed with water directly via pipe to the 'soil' surface.

CHAPTER 4

LIGHT CONSTRAINTS

> 'The position best suited for the erection of the greenhouse is one that is dry, exposed on the east, south and west sides, but, if possible, sheltered on the north... moreover, should have the front of fair height, so that the upright glass may catch as much of the obliquely slanting rays of the sun in winter as may be possible.'
>
> Isabella Beeton, *Mrs Beeton's Garden Management* (2008)

The siting of the greenhouse or polytunnel is vital. Place it where it can get the maximum of available light throughout the day to gain the maximum growing time – making sure you have accounted for winter sun as well as summer. To compensate for poor light – if you are inclined to grow crops through the seasons, or your growing season is short – it is advisable to install 'grow lights'.

Any protective hedge or wall will be under the same influence. It will have shade thrown on it and will act as a shade to other parts of the garden. It is always an important consideration when installing a structure or planting line, what effect it will have on the wider garden. A hedge, for example, will not only rob the soil of nutrient and water as it grows, but it will cause other plants to lose light if it is planted anywhere except on a north aspect.

Plants and Their Reaction to Light

Aside from photosynthesis, many plants have evolved with very specific light conditions and will move or grow, in a manner, in order to achieve their maximum potential. By growing in a certain direction, or growing tall to overcome shade, a plant is not incapable of helping itself. However, as it is always the gardener that creates the space, it is up to the gardener to understand that space and plant accordingly. For example, it is worthwhile remembering that a begonia needs a certain amount of light to produce flower buds. This means that artificial light can aid growth, as well as encourage early flowering. However, if you also own an African violet (which need 14 hours of darkness to encourage flowering), then you will have problems in the same setting.

The Effects of Too Much Sunlight

Light from the sun, whilst logically beneficial, can and will have an adverse effect under glass. Known for many years as 'scorch', the seemingly damaging process in plants is now recognized as a defence mechanism. According to Graham Fleming of Berkeley University, plants that receive too much sunlight react

A simple example of tropism. These Thai basil (*Ocimum basilicum* var. *thyrsiflora*) seedlings are growing towards the light on a kitchen windowsill.

by producing a member of the carotenoid family known as zeaxanthin. A defensive reaction, this molecule transfers an electron to chlorophyll, making it incapable of functioning properly – the positively charged zeaxanthin combines with the negatively charged chlorophyll, dispersing any excess energy as heat. Ultimately, the process, if left unchecked, destroys the plant (it is unable to move from the sun unless transported by the gardener elsewhere).

NB The process is switched off if a cloud passes momentarily across the sun.

Scorch is a problem that many plants suffer when given an ill-thought position or shading is inadequate. As the climate changes, this will become more evident.

Light and Photosynthesis

Photosynthesis is the process in which a plant makes food utilizing available carbon dioxide, water and light. It takes place inside structures within leaf cells known as chloroplasts.

Chloroplasts contain pigments known as chlorophylls, a green pigment that absorbs energy via sunlight to convert carbon dioxide and water to create a sugar, glucose, which is then used as a food source for the whole plant. It is green because it absorbs red and blue light, reflecting green and yellow. Energy from visible light is absorbed by these pigments initiating photosynthesis. However, each chloroplast has a narrow range of energy levels that they can absorb. Visible red light is the lowest energy that can raise an electron to an excited quantum state. On the flipside, if the energy is higher than visible blue light – ultra-violet – it will physically tear the molecules apart, causing bleaching. Therefore, plant pigments only absorb a wavelength range of 700–400nm, which is known as the photosynthetically active radiation.

Understanding Pigments

Many pigments exist within plants and each has evolved to absorb certain wavelengths. Pigments reflect back the wavelengths they cannot absorb, creating both beauty and interest to humans but also inefficiencies to the plant. Carotenoids, and more importantly chlorophylls, are the major classes of pigments in plants – each class has multiple types of pigment molecules. In plants there are four chlorophylls: a, b, c and d. The most pertinent to the gardener are chlorophyll a and chlorophyll b, which are found in higher plant chloroplasts. A much larger group of pigments are carotenoids – mostly found in fruit such as capsicum/bell pepper (β-carotene) or tomato (lycopene). These pigments are extremely efficient for two reasons. The first is to dispose of excess energy, dissipating it as heat – when a leaf or fruit is exposed to full sun, enormous amounts of energy are processed, and if that energy is not controlled, then significant damage is done (like in human skin with melanin). The second use of carotenoid is to advertise ripeness to seed dispersers.

Each type of pigment can be identified by its place on the 'absorption spectrum' – the specific wavelength it absorbs from visible light (*see* graph). If one looks at the graph for chlorophyll a, chlorophyll b and a carotenoid, such as β-carotene, one gains a wider understanding of the peaks and troughs of absorption and how it makes the plant more efficient. Chlorophyll a absorbs light from either end of the light spectrum, but not green. Chlorophyll b has a similar absorption rate. Both are responsible for a plant appearing green. Therefore, because green is reflected it makes chlorophyll appear green. Carotenoids absorb the blues and reds, reflecting greens, yellows and oranges. Plant breeders have played with these genetics to produce other colours, which create less efficiency in the plant but more pleasure to collectors.

Therefore, it is safe to assume that all the photosynthetic organisms in your care have a mixture of pigments; using them, the plant can absorb energy from a wider spectrum. However, not all plants come from areas with full sunlight. Some (many indoor plants) grow in competition for light in their natural habitat. For example, plants that have adapted for the rainforest floor must, as a matter of survival, be adapted to absorb any light that reaches it. For the same reason, variegation – a most attractive trait to some gardeners – creates inefficiencies that the plant will try to reverse.

A plant that is becoming a common hedge is *Photinia × fraseri*. Whilst attractive, its leaves are ultimately very inefficient, and its overuse results in increased problems with fungal and bacterial attacks.

In this instance, it is quite common for a plant to try to 'revert' to its natural state, increasing its efficiency to optimum levels.

Types of Natural Shade

Many plants, given the correct care, have the ability to adapt. However, some will not adapt to less light. The word shade is, therefore, a key element of growing and is measured at midsummer. Bear in mind, midwinter

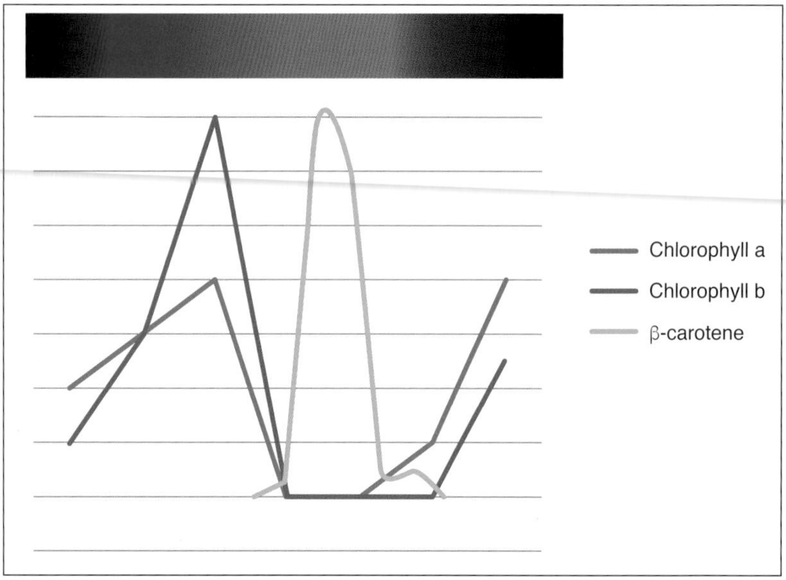

The absorption spectrum (simplified).

Natural shade can be a hindrance or a benefit for many reasons – not just access to light, but also access to water.

would be a better time to judge certain plantings (as with grass used as hedging) – an aspect without direct sunlight in midwinter leads to root-rot and other maladies. To understand the terminology, consult Table 3.

Helping a Plant Adapt to More Light

If the plant you have purchased has been growing in conditions with limited light, it is best that you give the specimen time to adapt. Therefore, expose the plant to increasing levels of direct light over the course of weeks.

NB Some species are not adapted to sit in full sun (*see* 'The Effects of Too Much Sunlight').

Artificial Shading

Shading needn't be expensive. Used well, and used correctly, it is a simple way to reduce damage to the plants within (*see* Chapter 5).

Table 3 Types of shade

Deep shade	Usually refers to the space under conifers, hedges or in the lee of houses or buildings. If there is no direct sun for more than two hours a day, this is associated with heavy shade. Take into consideration rain penetration.
Moderate shade	An area that receives three hours of direct sunlight. This may be areas in winter but not summer, so one must take into consideration sitting wet with no dry period for disease prevention.
Dappled shade	Sunlight diffused through the canopy of broadleaved or deciduous trees. This type of light is the most pertinent when dealing with tropical and sub-tropical house plants, which are mostly understorey plants.
Partial shade	Sites that receive between three and six hours of direct sunlight. The midday sun supplies much more light than at other times, so influences the classification to one of light shade. Bear in mind that the evening sun is warmer than the morning sun, so will affect the plants much more.
Light shade	A site that is open to the sky, but is under the influence of a hedge or wall. Take into consideration rain penetration.
Full sun	An area that gets more than six hours of direct sunlight at midsummer.

Ask an Expert

How do you counterbalance a need for shade with a need to keep light at a maximum?

Use shade cloth that can be opened and closed, as and when needed, i.e. pull shading over (or install automatic system to do it for you) at warmest parts of the day and open when shading is no longer needed. Shade cloth comes in different grades, i.e. 20 per cent, 50 per cent, 80 per cent, so choose best suited one for plants that are being grown. If an automated system is used, make sure to program it correctly! The shading can be programmed to shade greenhouses at a set light level (e.g. 150W/m^2 though light can be measured in different units such as W/m^2, footcandles, lux, lumens) and can be incremental (i.e. 10 per cent shade cloth closed at 100W/m^2 or 20 per cent at 120W/m^2 etc.). There are also greenhouse paints available (typically white but sometimes pinkish), usually applied in spring to shade greenhouses over summer and can be easily removed (some even wash away naturally over time) in autumn with citric acid or similar.

Scott Taylor, Conservatories Manager,
Kew Botanic Gardens

Plastic shade netting in place on the outside of the growing space. Whether it be paint or fabric, shading is an important aspect of every glasshouse. This greenhouse is made from polycarbonate and steel and, though usable, it is evidence that light structures struggle during winter storms. Therefore, make sure any extra fixings are suitable for the building structure. Private garden

Helpful Hint

It is worth noting that a viable alternative to those advertised – if you need a quick fix – is simple net curtains. Whilst not designed to be used in a horticultural setting, they can offer some shade for those plants less tolerant to harsh sun. However, any cloth inside the space will collect condensation, so will need to be checked regularly and washed.

In some instances, shading is not just against the sun. Frosts and rain can be an issue. These problems are not difficult to resolve, but need careful planning.

As described by Scott Taylor at Kew, there is a variety of adequate removable shading materials. The most common is glass paint, with the most obvious downside – the higher the structure, the more awkward the application. In other structures, such as polytunnels, most are naturally shaded due to the opaque plastic used.

Light Throughout the Year

In recent years, university research departments have become increasingly involved in production efficiency – modelling accurately year after year savings on energy usage to the extent that there is now annually a 2 per cent saving in food production globally.

White light, as 'discovered' by Newton and later expanded upon by Jean-Paul Marat, is broken by diffraction into seven visible colours. These are: red, orange, yellow, green, blue, indigo and violet. Of these colours, only two are most useful for plants to use in their processes, these being blue and red. Individually, blue light is by far the most effective at helping a plant grow – it being most easily absorbed for the photosynthetic processes to take place. Red light is most useful in making a plant flower and is also key in seed germination, root growth and bulb development. Therefore, in order to make efficiencies, it makes sense that any artificial light combines these two wavelengths as one light.

NB It must be noted that it is not simply a case of *any* blue or *any* red light, each must be a specific wavelength to aid growth – the wrong light can have adverse reactions.

Without going into the complexities of de Broglie-Bohm's 'pilot wave' theory, quantum coherence or the effects of shortened wavelengths on photon acceleration, RHS guidelines suggest that one seeks out lights that have the following wavelengths on the Kelvin scale: 4000K emit slightly redder tones, 7500K emit bluish light. For maximum benefit, a combination is advised.

ABOVE: Easily purchased 'stall clips' are adequate alternatives to professional fixings, if these are unavailable. (Protect your greenhouse surface with cloth or rubber to prevent damage.)

Growing underground. With no natural light and using hydroponics, successful horticulture can be achieved, even in the centre of huge cities such as London. Note the colour of light, which is a combination of both red and blue.

Artificial Light to Suit Your Purpose

The use of grow lights is now a very practical and affordable way to aid plants; they add to food production. The main benefits for using them are:

- To extend the growing season for plants.
- To start seedlings earlier in the year, so that they are stronger when planted out.
- To offer the correct growing conditions in areas with little or no light.
- To extend the cropping season of plants such as tomatoes.
- To potentially increase antioxidant properties of crops such as lettuce.

The key thing to remember with grow lights is to use the correct equipment. Domestic bulbs will not suffice; therefore, there are two main options:

The light array is visible at the growing Zero Carbon Farms underground facility. The combination of both red and blue light aids the development of both root and leaf.

A close up of a red LED light array.

- LED (light emitting diode). By far the most environmentally friendly and increasingly common, their energy expenditure is low. However, they may be more expensive to install in the initial setup
- HO (high output). These are known as T5 HO fluorescent tubes. According to the Royal Horticultural Society, these forms are highly efficient at producing adequate light to aid plant health, they are cheap and they are long-lasting.

There is a third option, which is HID (high intensity discharge). Being made from metal or sodium filaments, these lights give off intense heat and are unsuitable for any domestic setting.

Anecdotal evidence, as described to the author by the Scottish Horticulturist, Dave Allen:

> Grow lamps have a pretty limited range. It's a wet and cloudy day. The light meter reads 170 immediately below the light, 30cm away the reading is 52. As a control, a cauliflower growing on a windowsill (in winter) reads 11.

Four F32T8 32W fluorescent grow lamps.

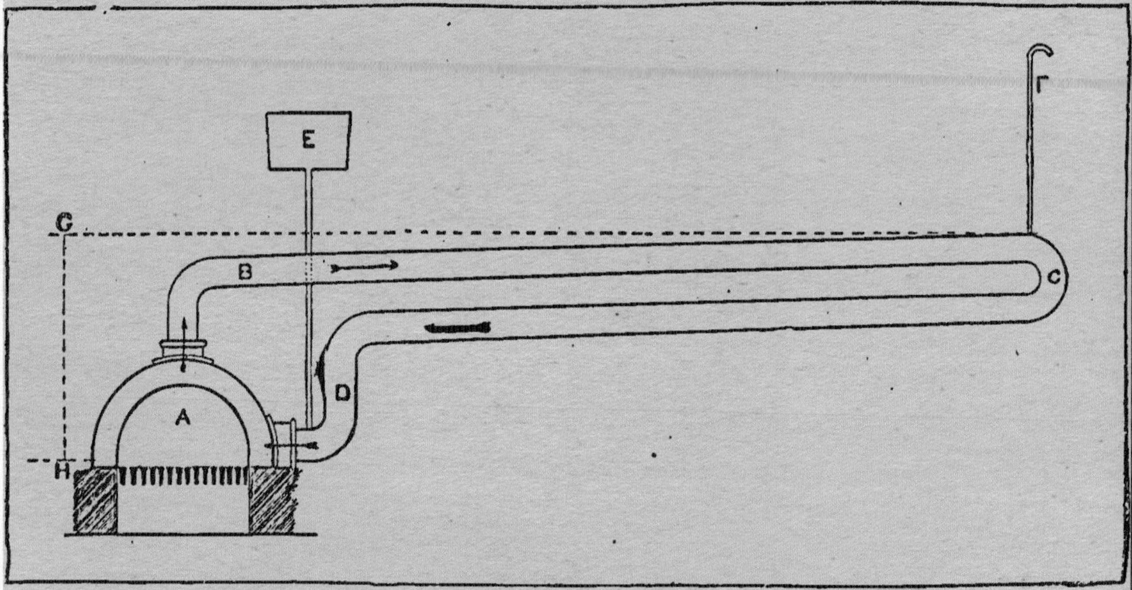

HEATING APPARATUS

A—The Boiler; *B-C*—The Flow Pipe; *C-D*—The Return Pipe; *E*—The Supply Cistern; *F*—The Air Pipe.

CHAPTER 5

TEMPERATURE CONTROL

'The mood in most of my friends' greenhouses is distinctly sad. The plants look unhappy – not through any deficiency in kindness on their owner's part but, quite simply because they are growing in too dry an atmosphere. Their leaves are matt and lustreless, hanging with a kind of pinched brittleness. And the owner's trouble is that, not knowing what a healthy plant should look like, he does not realize that anything is seriously amiss.

Christopher Lloyd,
The Well-Tempered Garden (1970)

Heat and Cold

The importance of temperature variability in your local environment is not to be underestimated. The UK as a whole has a mean winter temp of 8°C and mean summer temp of 22.4°C (data from the Met Office) and for the latitude is relatively mild. If one takes into account that the UK average is not the reality for many, differences are certain east to west, north to south. For example, rainfall is higher in the west than the east, meaning that winter temperatures are, on average, higher in Devon than Lincolnshire. Overall, these temperature differences will not create massive problems for the UK garden, if the correct procedures are followed. If your site is north-facing, there is some discussion as to whether it is advantageous. In winter, for example, the temperatures will never have a massive variation – frost will never lift over the course of the day, keeping the mean temperature constant. However, it also means that the sun never achieves any useful purpose. Therefore, it must be assumed that any north-facing room will have either a vastly reduced temperature or be heated to a mean temperature – increasing your costs. The advantage here is that you can plant a stand of evergreen trees or build an attractive screen to provide protection, relatively close (there will be no shade effect as the sun moves along the southern horizon), which will provide a more than adequate averaging microclimate. A south-facing room will be less affected by north winds, but the temperature variation will be greater as the sun is a generator of immense heat. Remember: a winter sun can provide a quite surprising amount of energy to a well-insulated greenhouse.

Plant Hardiness

Temperature affects everything from the smallest microbe to the tallest tree. Depending on the global region and altitude that the subject comes from, it will have adapted to that climate. Therefore, it is always important to understand those growing conditions, so that you can replicate them as near as possible. A plant from the Peruvian Amazon will not do well in an unheated greenhouse in Scotland, yet a plant from the Peruvian Cordillera Blanca will have few issues if given the right soil. Therefore, it is beneficial to understand certain terms that plant suppliers use when determining plants by 'hardiness'. If you are familiar with the United States Department of Agriculture (USDA) rating system, the UK exists somewhere between 7 and 10. The Royal Horticultural Society (RHS) has created a hardy rating scale (H), which will immediately tell you a plant's ability to withstand cold.

With global climates changing, some areas (such as the South-East UK) are expected to become more arid with higher summer temperatures and lower winter temperatures, whereas it is understood that the North and West of the UK and Ireland will see higher rainfall. What is certain for all regions is that the climate will have much more energy. It must also be stated here, this depends entirely on what happens to the North Atlantic Drift upon which these islands are so dependent for their average temperatures, but it is not within the remit of this book to postulate further.

Table 4 Hardiness scales

Hardiness	RHS scale	USDA scale	Description
Hardy	H7 to H4	USDA 5 to 9	There is a surprisingly large range of hardiness in this group. Some plants will easily take a temperature down to –20°C, whereas others will give up anywhere below 5°C. It is advised to always study your garden space and local climate before purchase to avoid disappointment.
Half-hardy	H3	USDA 10	Sensitive to cold, they are unlikely to survive a heavy frost. Best not to risk exposure to temperatures lower than 4°C but may withstand temps as low as –5°C for a short time. Can be overwintered outside in milder coastal areas or in an unheated greenhouse.
Tender	H2	USDA 11	Tolerant of cool temperatures (between 2 and 5°C) but will not take being frozen (including frozen soil). Best overwintered in a cool greenhouse or in a very sheltered position in a city such as London.
Warm temperate	H1c	USDA 11	Intolerant of temperatures falling below 5°C, these plants require a warm greenhouse or house to overwinter. They can be grown outdoors once any threat of frosts or low temperatures has passed.
Sub-tropical	H1b	USDA 12	Generally, these plants perform best as a houseplant and in a heated glasshouse, but can be taken outside in exceptionally warm periods. Read the growing conditions intently as many require a situation free from direct sunlight.
Tropical	H1a	USDA 13	A heated glasshouse or warm house is necessary to provide the best growing environment for these types of plant. They should not be taken into a cooler climate, as temperature and humidity variations will affect growth.

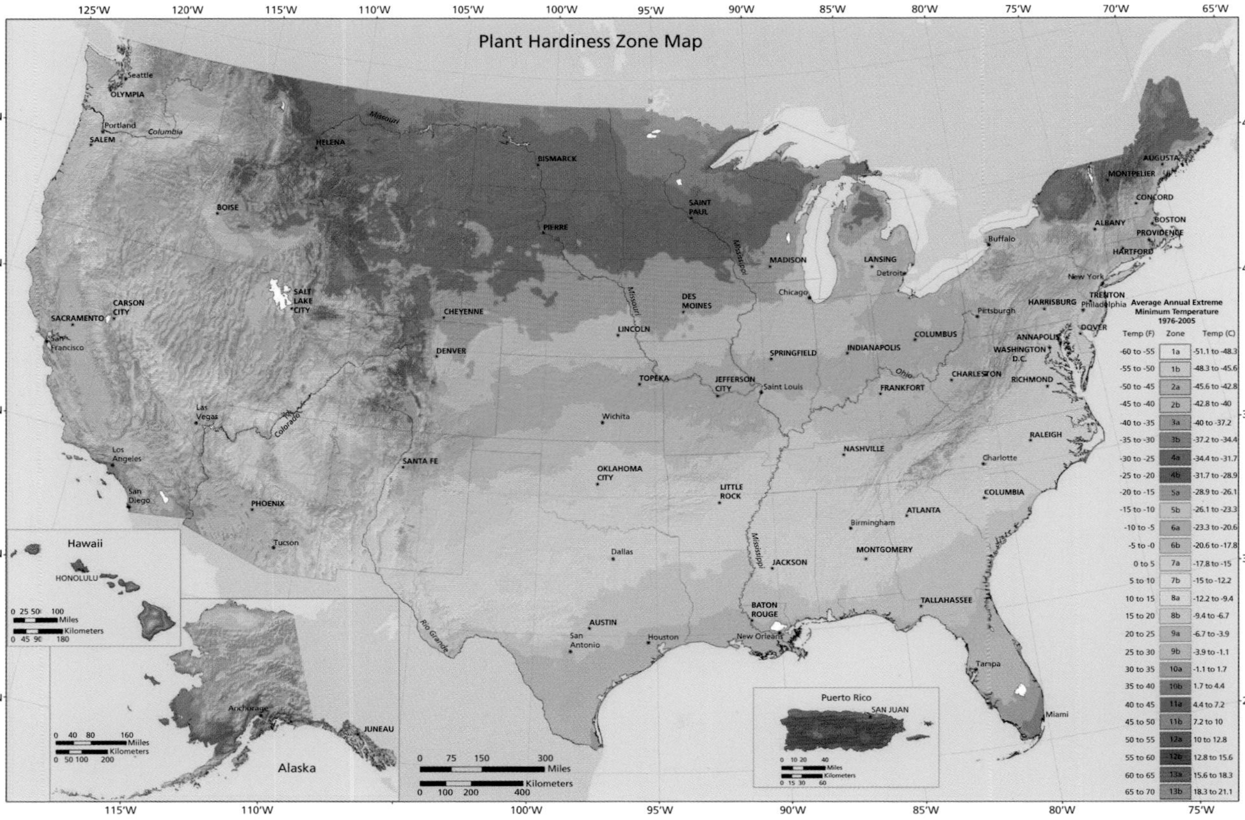

Temp (F)	Zone	Temp (C)
-60 to -50	1	-51.1 to -45.6
-50 to -40	2	-45.6 to -40
-40 to -30	3	-40 to -34.4
-30 to -20	4	-34.4 to -28.9
-20 to -10	5	-28.9 to -23.3
-10 to 0	6	-23.3 to -17.8
0 to 10	7	-17.8 to -12.2
10 to 20	8	-12.2 to -6.7
20 to 30	9	-6.7 to -1.1
30 to 40	10	-1.1 to -4.4
40 to 50	11	4.4 to 10
50 to 60	12	10 to 15.6
60 to 70	13	15.6 to 21.1

USDA hardiness zone map – USA.

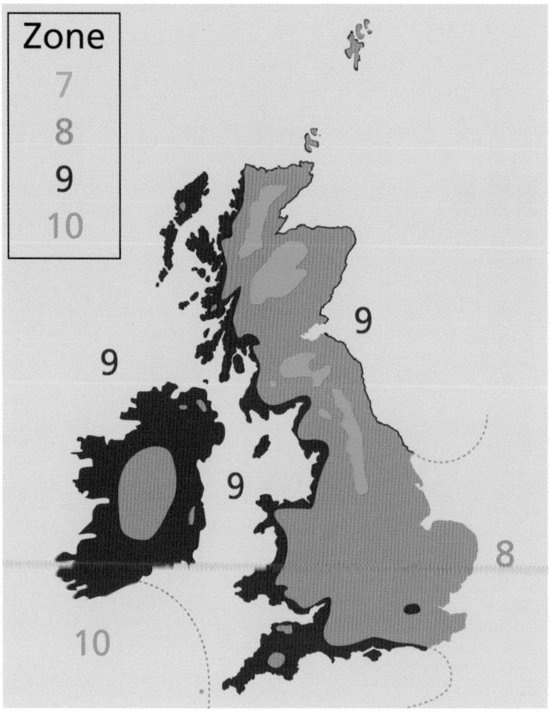

Greenhouse Classifications

In order to explore what can be achieved, you need to research what it is you want grow and then, using the hardiness list, experiment with the four main types of growing-house.

Unheated Greenhouse or Polytunnel

An unheated greenhouse is self-explanatory. Depending on site and situation, and following the guidance for insulating, the unheated greenhouse is best utilized as a simple frost free growing space for starting plants early into growth. If you are using it solely as a food production area, you can achieve remarkable results by paying attention to the weather and planting according to seasonal needs and availability of hardy seed. On a

TOP: USDA hardiness zone map – UK.

USDA hardiness zone map – Europe.

The unheated polytunnel or greenhouse is no different from a 'cool' growing-house in many respects and is by far the most common type in use. This is the interior of the large, unheated polytunnel at the Garden Gate Project. It is double-lined for heat efficiency, and can grow some quite remarkable plants in the space. If they have more delicate specimens, over the colder months, they install another temporary growing-house within the space and heat that. Remember, depending on where you are in the country, city, coast or countryside, the local climate may give you 3°C advantage on elsewhere.

small budget, an attractive display can be realized using hardy plants that will be encouraged to flower slightly earlier than those in the open garden. Otherwise, half-hardy perennials and shrubs can be stored over winter as the temperatures should not fall below 4°C.

The Cool Greenhouse

The concept of a cool greenhouse is simple. If the winter temperature does not fall below 10°C and frost is kept at bay, a much wider range of plants can be grown from simple sub-tropical house-plants to forcing bulbs or flowers. It is best if the greenhouse design has either wooden or brick walls to retain heat and affix the heating system to. Great care should still be taken to make sure that the upper temperatures do not climb too much, otherwise you will have problems with bud drop on some plants.

The Warm Greenhouse

The warm greenhouse should never fall below 13°C throughout the year. Ideal for raising a vast array of plants from those ordinarily hardy in the wider garden to more exotic species, the warm greenhouse holds many possibilities for year-round interest. By far the best approach is to dedicate areas to specific needs. Water tanks to keep the air humid are imperative, but excellent ventilation is also key.

The Tropical Greenhouse

Otherwise known as a stove house, the temperature should never fall below 21°C throughout the year.

The cool greenhouse. This glasshouse has been sited too close to an overhanging tree; thus, it loses morning light. However, a microclimate has been created that would keep it above freezing on all but the coldest of days. Temperature can be manipulated without the use of mechanical means in some instances, but the installation of electrical heating is not difficult. Having a brick or wooden base to the glasswork aids insulation on this type of house. It also has a potting shed, to store everything needed away from the plants.

The Princess of Wales Conservatory Kew. An example of a multitude of environments (ten) in one space, including a 'warm' climate. Heated by a series of underground hot-water pipes, and with ventilation and humidity controlled by computer, the individual spaces are maintained to maximize growing conditions.

The interior of the Princess of Wales Conservatory, Kew. The ventilating windows are wide open even in late November.

Careful note should be taken that in these conditions, pest and disease are a constant threat, so good hygiene practice is imperative. Sizeable rainwater tanks are also a necessary function of any such house to provide the moist atmosphere required and the high water needs of most rainforest plants. The soil should be free-draining and soil-heating elements would be beneficial. The plants available to grow in this environment are extensive, from the exquisite jade vine to bromeliads such as pineapple.

How to Enhance the Growing Conditions Under Glass

Insulation

It is often recommended that the greenhouse and poly-tunnel be insulated against the worst of winter weather. One such tool recommended by manufacturers is horti-cultural bubble-wrap. The polytunnel is a more complex issue and it has been recommended by some experts that in the initial build you double-layer your structure if your area is particularly exposed to hard weather.

Another method available to the gardener is horti-cultural fleece. Light and simple to use, it can be placed across the borders or staging to protect plants that you feel are more likely to be affected by the cooling night-time temperatures.

Heating

Heating a greenhouse can be a complex issue, depending on what you have chosen to grow and what the capabilities of the space are. There are many meth-ods of doing so; the most common today is via electrical means.

The palmhouse at The Royal Botanic Gardens, Kew. An exceptionally fine example of a tropical house. Heated by hot-water pipes, this house is designed to maintain temperatures that suit the plants within throughout the year.

BELOW: Bubble-wrap insulation needn't be expensive and is easily installed.

Helpful Hint

Before installing any form of insulation, work out how you are going to attach it. Suction cups can be purchased from haberdashery suppliers, but tape can be used if suitable to use on your frame material. Measure the area needed – cut to size rather than trying to do it by eye. Any ventilation points will need a separate piece so that it can be utilized should the need arise. Do not seal the entire structure – leave some air-circulation points free.

Be Warned

If you intend on heating your greenhouse, or have inherited a heated greenhouse, it is important you get the advice of a specialist first. Make sure the equipment you are using is safe and in good working order.

NB Using flammable liquid heaters used to be quite common, however this is not recommended for the following reasons: they give off toxic fumes (to both humans and plants), they adversely increase moisture and humidity in the space, they add to our global carbon footprint and they need to be attended to regularly.

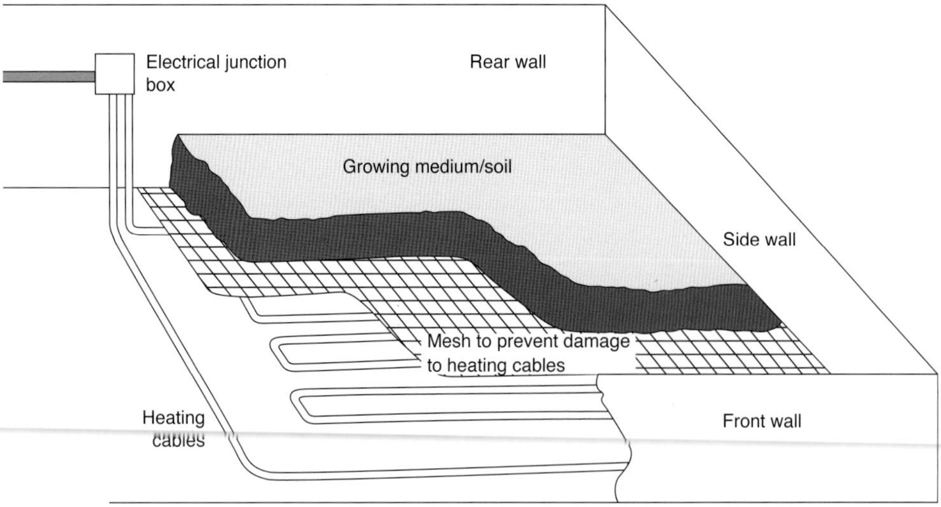

A schematic of undersoil heating. This gives the gardener the added option of earlier cropping. Always consult a professional when installing electrics.

Ask an Expert

Is heating a greenhouse a complex undertaking?

Heating a greenhouse allows you to extend your growing season. In a small glasshouse, less than 15 square metres, with lower temperature requirements, a fan heater is probably the most sensible choice. If size or temperature requirements are greater, then a more complex system is required. Heating systems from convection of heat work from a hot body in a similar fashion to a radiator system in a house. This provides a gentle convection current around the glasshouse, which is kinder to the plants than blowing hot air at them and drying out the leaves and spreading diseases. The heat can be provided electrically or via a hot-water system. We would normally recommend electric up to about 8kW and hot-water systems above this. The reason for this is that most domestic electrical supplies will only accommodate an 8kW load. A hot-water system is usually based around an oil or gas boiler.

Kitty Yarrow, Alitex Greenhouses

Electric Heaters

Electric heaters are currently the most environmentally friendly option. If you are looking at generating your own electricity supply via solar panels, it may be some time before a suitable system is generally available. According to industry experts, running electrical heating from solar systems is very inefficient and requires very large systems at high cost (if you want reliability, you would also need to have a backup generator). There are three main types of heaters that can be used. First, tubular radiators that can be fixed to a wall – the heat as in a radiator rising and circulating. The second is a fan heater. These should be placed in the centre of the greenhouse, making sure to never allow the air to blow directly on to plants. The third is warming the soil via pipes, cables or elements, which are most useful when placed directly underneath or in the growing medium, especially in propagators.

A viable alternative is a solar thermal system (*see* Chapter 6 for one version), which warms water utilizing the sun's natural heat, keeping the cool greenhouse above a certain temperature. By attaching an immersion heater or conventional boiler, the water can be heated up to provide a warmer climate.

Gas Heaters

Gas heaters utilize either the natural gas mains or propane gas in bottles and are a throwback to times when

A fan heater is now one of the most common heaters to purchase. They are useful in smaller spaces, though, if the insulation is wrong, they will be expensive. Try to purchase one that also aids airflow in warmer weather.

it was acceptable to burn carbon-based fuels. The positives are that they produce carbon dioxide, which plants use during the day, and they are moveable. However, on the negative side, they also produce high levels of humidity and need ventilation in order to run safely. They also should never be left alone, limiting the gardener's scope.

Boiler

For larger, enclosed spaces, which are over 4m wide and 3m long – or greenhouses being purposed for hotter climates – a boiler is a better choice. Solid fuel, gas or electric boilers connected to water-filled pipes provide a reliable heating system. If you are installing a gas boiler connected to the mains, make sure it is one that can be modified to run on hydrogen. The boiler should always be positioned outside the greenhouse under protective covering, the pipes running into the greenhouse and around the perimeter wall. The good points to this system are: thermostatically controlled, slow to cool if the boiler stops and good heat distribution. The bad points are that they cannot be used effectively in smaller spaces and they are slow to respond in situations when temperatures change rapidly. They are also expensive to install and expensive to maintain.

Ways of Manipulating Local Temperatures

Something many people don't realize when they build structures or utilize protective measures is that they

Electrical heaters attached to the wall under the staging. Working on the same principle as domestic radiators, they keep the air at a mean temperature. Again, insulation is required to keep the heating efficient.

are actively affecting the local climate. If, for example, you put plastic netting across a seedling border to protect from birds, you are raising the temperature under that netting by about 10 per cent. Equally, a wall will reflect heat, lifting temperatures and making an area less prone to frosts. If, on the other hand, you are finding an area is 'too hot', plants such as lambs ears (*Stachys byzantina*) have been proven to reduce local temperatures by up to 2°C when planted *en masse*. A green wall has an equal effect and aids moisture retention if planted in a sheltered area. Digging a trench, adding fresh manure then covering with a thin layer of soil, will create a 'hot bed' – the chemical reaction of the manure breaking down will create heat and encourage plants, such as strawberries, to grow, flower and ripen earlier. Lastly, a large body of water will affect temperatures, generally stabilizing the local air to a mean temperature – thus seaside gardens often grow less-hardy plants with impunity throughout the year.

Thermometers

As part of your journey in gardening, you will find it worthwhile to know the temperature – especially within the enclosed environment of a greenhouse or polytunnel. The most useful tool in any structure is a maximum and minimum thermometer. For accurate reading, it should be placed out of direct sunlight and in a place where air can circulate. This type of thermometer works on the basis of having two columns, each equipped with small needles that are pushed as the temperatures rise or fall, remaining in position to

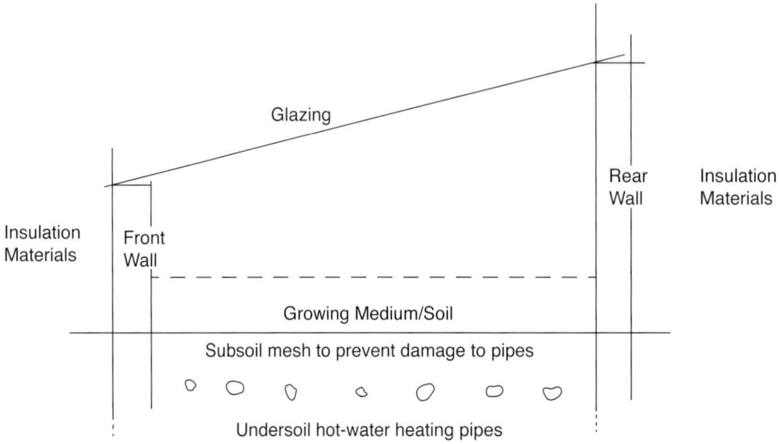

ABOVE LEFT: An industrial heating unit provides the necessary warmth to plants as they are prepared to go to market in early spring.

A sketch of under-soil heating via water pipes for a cold-frame or similar. Utilizing a boiler system, heated pipes can transfer either hot steam or hot water beneath the growing beds or the greenhouse. The same principle can warm a greenhouse with the pipes above ground.

A misting propagation unit with under-soil elements. Propagation is not difficult to get right but is an art in itself – depending on the plant being propagated and what your aim is. Always follow hygiene protocols.

indicate the highs and lows in the previous 24 hours. Take a note of your readings and adjust the thermostat or ventilators accordingly (*see* 'Temperature Control and Ventilation').

A more up-to-date method of temperature reading is the digital thermometer. Following the same principle as the traditional thermometer, it is always advisable to get the best you can afford, making sure that it is not manufactured poorly, that the casing is sealed from water and that the battery compartment is watertight.

Be Warned

The traditional method was via a mercuric thermometer, but this is now banned for sale as mercury is incredibly toxic. It is a strong recommendation of this book for the reader to make sure that any such instrument is 'mercury free' and that any old mercury thermometers are disposed of in the correct manner.

Shading a Greenhouse Correctly

Light is vital to plant health and growth. Without it plants suffer (*see* Chapter 4). However, the sun is an incredibly powerful source of energy – too much can cause serious issues for your plants. The majority of books will recommend that you shade the greenhouse throughout the hotter months to avoid plant scorch; they will also advise that it is useful to keep the temperature from rising too high. Your aim is to provide just enough to suit the plants within – not too much, not too little. It is recommended that you understand the botany of your plants, observing the space as one would any other part of the garden and placing plants according to their light needs.

A digital thermometer is a better tool than the traditional gauge, but only if properly installed.

The shading in the alpine house, Kew. It was designed to provide the plants within with the dry, cool and windy conditions they need to thrive. The shape of the structure creates a 'stack effect', drawing the hot air out. Beneath the structure, the air is cooled and recirculated, the glazing allowing 90 per cent of sunlight to penetrate.

Blinds are not uncommon, but more often than not they are left out of any initial design as a costly addition. They are most useful on the outside of any structure to prevent condensation and temperature build-up – unlike interior blinds. They come in various forms from textiles, such as hessian, to wooden or metal slats. If possible, the blinds should be suspended on runners or rails above the glass to allow the absorbed heat to dissipate in the air. When not needed, they can simply be rolled back up. Be aware that the cloth variety will need to be stored in winter months to prevent mould build-up and they are vulnerable to wind damage. An additional benefit of the blinds can be as a useful protection against frosts.

Plastic shading is by far the most commonly purchased alternative to blinds. One major fault is that, in the majority of cases, this is either a dark-green or black plastic. In both instances, this is illogical because dark colours absorb heat rather than repel it. Therefore, they do not lower temperatures, although they do act as a shade from the sun's rays.

Shading paints are a popular choice, as they are easily painted on using a brush. Easily purchased from garden centres and similar stores, they are an ideal choice for the smaller greenhouse. White in colour, they can be bought as a concentrate and diluted or ready mixed. Many older books give a recipe for making your own using quick-lime, which is not recommended, as quick-lime is extremely caustic. Aside from this, another basic form of shade in the greenhouse is white polythene sheeting, which can be attached to the inside of the greenhouse (the method being entirely up to the gardener). This is suitable for year-round shade, where you are growing dormant fruit, or plants that cannot take direct sunlight. The downside is that it encourages moisture build-up, so ventilation is important.

Damping-Down

It is essential to keep the greenhouse air humid. Damping-down is a procedure that is mostly used in warmer months and involves wetting, with water, the inside of the walls, floors and staging at least once a day – depending on the weather. The hotter and drier the atmosphere, the more the process will have to be followed. Biologically, damping-down reduces the transpiration rate of plants, which in turn reduces the need to water. It is always worth noting that the great majority of plants do not like excessively high temperatures. In order to cool air rapidly, the water used in the damping-down process needs energy to evaporate – thus, any excess heat in the air is taken in the process of evaporation, cooling the air to acceptable levels.

NB It is also important that shading and ventilation are included in your routines to allow airflow and reduce UV damage.

Temperature Control and Ventilation

To ensure healthy plant growth, you will, at some point, have to work out how to control the temperature in the space you have chosen. The simplest

Damping-down regulates the air moisture levels, reducing plant stresses.

method is to utilize vents known at ventilators: either via a door – as in the polytunnel – or via specially designed windows that open in the greenhouse. However, too much airflow can cause problems. According to Isabella Beeton in her book, *Mrs Beeton's Garden Management* (2008):

> The utmost care should be taken to prevent draught, especially a thorough draught passing right through the house. To ensure this, ventilators should never be opened at opposite sides of the house at the same time – that is to say the top and bottom ventilators, or front and back ventilators, should never be opened at the same time.

Helpful Hint

It is advisable to make sure your structure is suitably equipped. In a greenhouse, a ventilator every 2m (6ft) is adequate in the present climate, but this may have to be rethought. In a polytunnel or crug, it is advisable to have a doorway at both ends to allow airflow directly through the space – making sure that the plants are not directly affected by strong draughts. Thus, original siting is key. In either structure, the addition of a dissipating fan in the roof, or an extractor fan opposite the doorway, may also be prudent.

NB Make sure all additions do not affect the integrity of the overall structure.

Summer is a different proposition to winter. Your problem is not heat conservation, but how to dissipate it. From February all the way through to late November, it will not be unusual for a small amount of sun to heat the greenhouse quite rapidly. As the sun reaches its zenith in the middle months, this welcome heat will become an unwelcome burden. If you have chosen to site your structure well and included adequate ventilation as integral to the design, then your problems will be minimized.

Types of Ventilator in a Greenhouse

In a polytunnel, where doors are the main ventilator, it may be advised to install a weighted fabric screen to allow air but not wind to flow through the space. For the greenhouse, there are two main types of ventilator that you will come across. The solid pane, opened by a hinge and a casement stay (sometimes, you will come across a more ornate system but the principle is the same). This allows the window to be opened to varying degrees by simple action of a lever. The second type is a louvre window, which is found most in aluminium structures. Whilst this system is useful – it is relatively

Ask an Expert

How do you keep heat and humidity satisfactory without encouraging devastating pathogens such as fungi?

Ventilating at the most appropriate time of day helps to keep a buoyant and fresh atmosphere under cover. During winter, a house may only be ventilated for a few hours but this will be done when the daily temperatures are at their highest. Where composts in beds and pots are wet, humidity levels can be kept high by watering hard surfaces only, which will keep water away from plants and help against plant pathogens. Winter temperatures under cover are lowered and a balancing lowering of the amount of water given will also assist in not creating negative conditions for plants while their metabolism is at low levels.

Brendan Sayers, Glasshouse Foreman,
National Botanic Gardens, Glasnevin, Ireland

The interior of Glasnevin Tropical House.

easy to replace existing solid panes for as many ventilators as you feel you need – they have the downside of not fitting snuggly, allowing adverse draughts in winter.

Automatic Ventilation

A relatively cheap investment, if you have busy schedules and leave your glasshouse unattended for extended periods, is an automatic ventilator arm; it is worthwhile

The bonsai house, Kew. A simple house, the ventilators are operated manually.

Shading and ventilation in use on aluminium greenhouses in Kent. Louvre ventilating windows can clearly be seen (though blocked), as well as standard roof vents. The shading is two-fold: paint and shade netting hanging from wires (inside). Private garden.

A Bayliss automatic ventilator arm. Easily bought in good retailers and not difficult to adjust according to needs.

BELOW RIGHT: Fan in a commercial greenhouse. These aid the movement of air to help cooling and reduce prevalence of disease. They are excellent in polytunnels, as well as under glass.

Ask an Expert

In simple terms, can you outline ventilation?

Ventilation is a critical part of growing under glass. A combination of roof and side vents creates a 'chimney effect' inside the greenhouse that encourages air circulation and prevents unhelpful through drafts. The number of opening vents is designed according to the needs of each individual greenhouse to give the optimum level of ventilation. On larger greenhouses, vent depth can be increased accordingly and electric motors added for precision control. Vents are positioned in one vertical side in a bank (or banks, depending on the size and shape of the greenhouse). They are 0.9m deep (3ft) and operated manually using a traditionally styled solid cast-aluminium lever and link system. The length of the bank(s) of side vents will depend on the length of the greenhouse. Vents in the roof are also set in bank(s) and 0.6m (2ft) deep. On greenhouses up to 3.5m wide, they are operated by temperature-sensitive openers. These consist of a piston filled with synthetic wax that expands, as the external temperature heats up, to open the vent. As the external temperature cools, the wax contracts and the vents close. Once set, they can be left to operate automatically. The openers are often referred to by the manufacturer's name 'Bayliss'. Greenhouses 4.5m wide will have roof vents 1.2m (4ft) deep. Due to the increased weight of the vent, they will need to be operated by an electric motor.

Kitty Yarrow, Alitex

and can be fitted to all ridge and side ventilators as needed. Widely available from greenhouse retailers, the principle is simple. Each unit is 'powered' by an expanding liquid and pneumatic tension – as temperatures rise, the lever forces open the vent, as temperatures cool the liquid cools, shrinks and the lever arm retracts.

The benefit of this system is that no external power is needed; the unit can also be preset to open at set temperatures from about 14°C.

Different Climates

Once the gardener is adept at providing a suitable climate for a multitude of hardy fruit and flowers, they may consider expanding their repertoire to providing an adequate shelter to more exacting plants, such as those that live in the deep jungle or high altitude. The best thing to do in such circumstances is to seek out a local club of fellow enthusiasts who will be happy to share their knowledge. Following is a brief guide.

Growing Alpines

Alpines are primarily high-altitude plants used to relatively poor conditions – they need free-draining soil. Whilst they are hardy plants, withstanding very cold temperatures and high UV levels, they do not like to sit wet. Therefore, many will grow outside in the summer, but in the winter they need a glasshouse with plenty of ventilation – both above and below the staging. Always ventilate on the leeward side, as draughts will cause issues.

Growing Succulents

Remove yourself from the assumption that succulents are not an exacting group of plants – it is assumed that they live in dry and arid conditions, but they are found growing in temperate coastal areas and sub-tropical rainforests. Adapted to cope with extremes of climate, they can adapt to areas with milder climates, high light intensity and irregular watering. The key to all is good drainage. In general, the two main demands of a succulent are warmth in spring, summer and autumn with good ventilation to avoid humidity. To circumvent winter damage, watering can be withheld entirely between November and early March – a period otherwise known as their 'resting period'. As long as the soil is dry, they can withstand quite cool temperatures. However, one key group, 'the mimicry' types, will require a different husbandry altogether. Plants from this group require high light, low humidity and low water to thrive.

Growing Orchids

The key with orchids is to understand their biology – it being the largest group of flowering plants on the planet. It is generally recommended that they be grown in a house entirely devoted to their cultivation, though some types such as *Coelogyne* and *Odontoglossum* of the montane ecosystems will thrive in a more general environment. The majority of orchids (about 70 per cent) are epiphytes – taking nutrient from the air and water. Not all orchids live in the tropics, need high humidity or flourish in the ready-made 'orchid bark compost' foisted upon the unwary amateur. It is also worth noting that the 'clear' pots provided are more a help to the nurserymen who produced them to check for root-rot and are not a necessary growing-aid. A readily available compost can be made utilizing dried bracken – a worthy substitute for the more expensive osmunda fibre. Some may do well with untreated charcoal, others will need limestone. The majority are 'understorey plants', so will not appreciate direct sun, shading being necessary even in winter – though they do need plenty of light, so anything that lowers light levels on dull days will be a problem (*see* Shading).

Temperatures vary as per species, but the majority on offer prefer a range between 13 and 16°C (make sure to be aware of any automatic ventilation systems

The display of succulents (and other plants) in the Tropical Britain nursery, Surrey. Requiring specific conditions, their watering and heating is carefully controlled so that they are kept at their optimum.

If you are intending on growing a wide variety of species, it may be best to divide the greenhouse into two: one being for cooler conditions and one for warmer. The simplest way to do this is by using a double-layered, heavy-gauge polythene sheet and soil-warming cables for the heated side. Be prepared to move the orchids about the space until optimum growing conditions are achieved, as those same growing conditions will always differ about the space – no matter how uniform you try to make it.

Staging is also a major factor. Unlike many greenhouse situations where the staging required must be of the single type and un-slated, it is recommended that the set-up be of the double type: the orchids sitting on upper, slated stages to accommodate light, the lower stage covered in gravel to accommodate humidity. In such environments, always follow strict hygiene routines, such as regularly cleaning tools with 70 per cent alcohol solutions.

Growing Vegetables

There is great pleasure to be had growing vegetables in a protected space or under cover – especially for those intending to achieve an all-year-round food supply or those aiming at 'early' cropping. The range of plants available is expansive and ever-increasing as the seed suppliers breed new varieties. The best way forward is to research and experiment. For example, leaf garlic from South Africa or Thai basil will need a sheltered winter, but can grow outside once frosts have passed. Always be sure of rotating the crops if you are growing directly in the soil, being aware of nutrient expenditure

that may be installed). A rapid loss of heat *will* cause issues. No definitive rules can be applied to the entire group, as the biology differs so greatly – some will require more frequent ventilation than others, but it is noted that none will appreciate draughts, so always open any ventilation on the leeward side.

ABOVE: Orchids growing in the Princess of Wales Conservatory, Kew. Whilst the space afforded at Kew offers plants with a habitat closer to their natural state, the domestic glasshouse can be designed sympathetically to imitate small pockets of the sub-tropical or even tropical zone.

Vegetables can be grown in most spaces, including those that you build yourself. This polytunnel was put together and used by the urban farm at Lambeth.

and salt build-up. Because you are intending to grow similar plants *en masse*, health and hygiene of the space is imperative. Prevention is always better than cure, making sure all imported plants or seed sourced has a good provenance.

Growing Fruit

Depending on the size of the space you have, growing fruit is highly rewarding. At the most basic level, cordon, espalier and fan-trained trees against a brick wall are an excellent way of utilizing a space. A fruit cage is also highly rewarding and requires relatively low maintenance over the year, if mulches and a weeding regime are applied. In certain UK cities, the protective environment of surrounding buildings has made it possible to successfully grow avocadoes outside throughout the year, so the opportunities for experimenting are ever-expanding. In cooler climates, a house dedicated to nectarines, apricots or citrus is a splendid addition to any grand enterprise, though great care must be taken to prevent infestation of certain pests.

Growing Ferns

Ferns generally prefer an environment without direct sunlight, so a north-facing lean-to is recommended. However, there is considerable confusion in the mind of the non-botanist gardener between the 10,000 true ferns and the so-called ferns such as asparagus. If you want to indulge your fascination with this outstanding family of plants, it is advisable to join a Pteridological Society. It is possible to grow ferns successfully in a normal environment as long as they are protected from the scorching rays of full sun (*see* Shading). The staging they sit on needs to be solid and layered with shingle in order that moisture remains constant – though some will do exceptionally well in the deep shade underneath!

Minimum temperatures for temperate ferns should not fall below 4°C in winter, though tender and hothouse ferns won't cope below 16°C. Frequent syringing to maintain air moisture is necessary, but be aware, all greenhouse ferns have a period of dormancy when they require less – they must never dry off completely though. As in the orchid house, ventilation is necessary, most usefully below the staging. Damp-down to maintain humidity, as required.

With Global Warming a Factor, is the Sun Hotter or More Luminous?

It is vital that any serious gardener gains some understanding of global climate change. The short answer to the question posed is 'yes but, no' – at least, not in any way that would concern gardening for about half a billion years. According to NASA, the sun's irradiance has fallen since 1880, but global temps have risen inexorably. However, there is concern that UV exposure increased by roughly 6 per cent over the last fifty years of the twentieth century, stabilizing in the mid-1990s to current levels. This concerns horticulture most because the effects of strong and prolonged exposure to certain UV light is very damaging to the DNA of both

This glasshouse at Farringford is an excellent example of a house that can be utilized to grow fruit as well as service other needs within the garden.

The fern house, Christchurch Botanic Garden, Canterbury, New Zealand. Opened in 1955, it is an excellent example of a glasshouse dedicated to local flora in a natural setting. As you can see from the image, increased light is not the primary aim of the house. A stream, incorporated into the design, aids air moisture levels.

plants and animals, reducing growth and increasing vulnerability to disease. Whilst both UV-A and UV-B light are beneficial to a plant's growth – aiding photosynthesis – UV-B has the opposite effect if too intense. This has increased the most at both higher and lower latitudes (little change at the equator) resulting in a loss of photosynthetic efficiency by between 16 and 40 per cent, depending on the species. One noticeable result of the increased UV-B exposure is that flowering times can change dramatically, altering the life cycles of other species that rely on established biorhythms.

Of most interest is the seasonal variation across the globe. Whilst the southern hemisphere has the highest global increase overall of UV-B, mostly in the months between April and August, the northern hemisphere has the increase during the months from November to March. This obviously goes against the natural assumption that the summer months would be most damaging. Therefore, it is in the gardener's interest to ensure that their protective covering takes this into account (see Shading).

NB These months are generally more cloudy – being late autumn and winter – which reduces the UV-B effect 2 per cent from the overall increase of 6 per cent originally discussed. From the perspective of the wider garden biosphere, the impact has yet to be fully understood. It is acknowledged that bio-geochemical cycles and overall biodiversity will be affected.

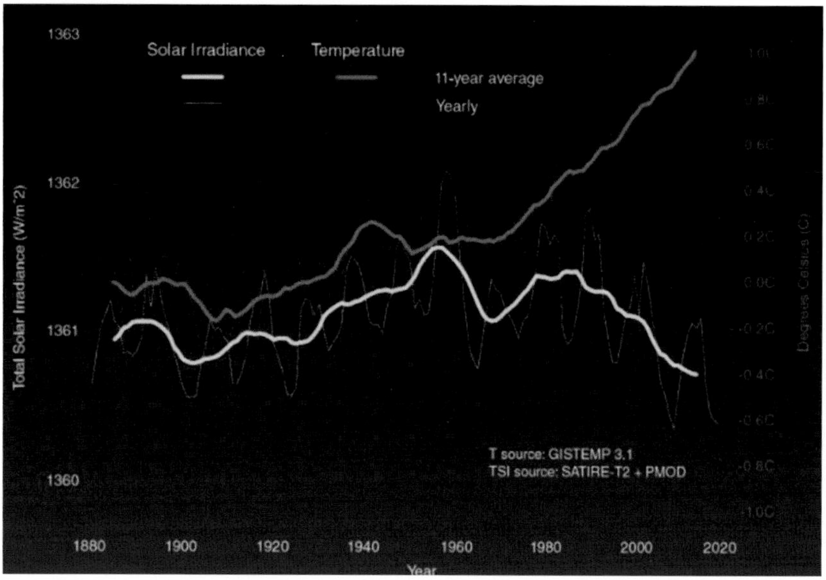

ABOVE: Solar irradiance has not increased, though it is clear that global temperatures have increased.

LEFT: A fern house needn't be made from glass. This house is at the Garden Gate Project in Margate. Utilizing the slatted wood design and retaining brick wall offers the plants within the shaded microclimate needed to flourish.

CHAPTER 6

THE IMPORTANCE OF SUSTAINABILITY

> 'Everything I have tried to do, and urge, over the past fifty years has been done with our children and grandchildren in mind, because I did not want to be accused by them of doing nothing except prevaricate and deny the problem.'
>
> Part of a speech made by HRH Prince Charles at the World Economic Forum, January 2020

What is Sustainability and Why is it Important?

It was once stated that if China became equal in living standards to those of Western Europe, there would physically not be enough natural resource to sustain the rest of the planet (*An Index of Possibilities. Energy & Power*. Chesterman et al., 1974) – an interesting anecdote that at this stage in the development of humankind, is quite pertinent. The continued mining of fresh resources, whilst a vast amount of useful material is dumped in large holes in the ground as 'useless', seems a remarkable situation to be in. Often this is because it is more expensive in monetary terms to recycle rather than collect new material – a solution based on an idea of 'cheap is profit' (i.e. given the need for 'constant growth' in the economies of the world, it can be assumed it is cheaper and more profitable to continue on the current path, ignoring the future consequences or seeing those consequences as an opportunity for growth once the expense is equalized with economic scarcity). The premise of sustainability is to check this mindset and introduce an idea of reuse rather than refuse with three pillars: economic, environmental and social.

Within the garden setting, sustainability is key to correcting our previous mistaken husbandry that insisted on chemical controls and tight regiment. Many professional gardeners are now following a more balanced ethic in order to achieve their aims of sustainability and, therefore, encourage a wider biodiversity into their spaces. One such garden is Audley End in Saffron Walden Essex. Run by English Heritage their aim is to create an historic garden, following more sustainable methods to achieve their goals.

From current literature, we can ascertain that there are three burgeoning crises that affect gardening in the twenty-first century: the first is a massive reduction in biodiversity; the second is the sheer weight of manufactured 'stuff' that is now heavier than all living things on the planet combined; the third is the climate deterioration caused by an increase in 'greenhouse gases' such as carbon dioxide and methane. At the time of writing this book, there has been much discussion on the implications caused by the ongoing 'Anthropocence

Audley End walled garden. Mulching for water retention can be seen on the espalier trees.

Ask an Expert

What sustainable practices do you follow at Audley End House?

- Integrated Pest Management – use of biological controls, cultural controls – best practice in maintenance throughout the year (e.g. pruning, weeding, mulching).
- Locally sourced natural materials for plant supports, e.g. willow/birch/hazel structures (supplied by Essex Wildlife Trust).
- Reusing materials each year, e.g. netting, fleece, rope, etc.
- Propagation of stock plants to boost our collection.
- Biodegradable punnets, bags for selling our produce to local outlets that use predominantly electric vehicles and serve the local area.
- Water wisely and properly (deeply).
- Considering environmental factors when selecting plants – right plant right place.
- Green manures (where compost not possible/appropriate).
- Soil Association organic status.
- Compost – around 30 tonnes; can't produce more than 80 tonnes a year otherwise incur a charge (Environment Agency).
- Crop rotation.
- Mulching.
- Source primarily organic seeds, which tend to be open-pollinated.
- Try to incorporate seed-saving practices where possible/appropriate.
- Very low fertilizer use/Zero use of mechanical cultivation.
- No-dig beds – experimental.
- RootWave Electricide machine for weed control.

Kelly Fowler, Senior Kitchen Gardener,
Audley End House, English Heritage

Mass Extinction' and the 'Anthropogenic Climate Change'. According to scientists such as Daniel Rothman PhD of the Lorenz Center MIT, 'each mass extinction has created an entirely new global environment which further impacts the cycle'. With this in mind, governments across the globe are publishing large amounts of prediction data for the levels of future weather patterns, sea-level rises and changes to global, as well as local, environments. Many of those governments have also declared 'climate emergencies' – an acknowledgement that action must be undertaken in order to mitigate future issues arising from the situation. Accordingly, the most likely pattern for the planet is an increase in mean temperatures – which in layman's terms creates a cycle where more energy is put into the atmosphere. Thus storms will be more violent, droughts more intense, weather patterns more unpredictable. So, from a gardening point of view, it is imperative that any structures – be they organic or mineral – that create a protective microclimate are well-suited and well-designed for the coming changes. It also follows that it is better for the planet to utilize what is already manufactured, rather than encouraging the removal of yet more of the planet's dwindling resources, simply adding to the burden.

Ask an Expert

How do you think the predicted future climate will affect plant-life in the UK?

It is impossible to overstate the effect that climate change will have on the entire process of growing. Already in some parts of the world, growers are giving up on particular classes of plants that they have grown for many years. In general, and in most parts of the world, weather patterns will become more erratic. In 2014, our palmhouse was entirely destroyed by a freak tornado. In the southern part of the UK where we are based, summers are becoming hotter and drier. Heat-waves are now common. When these are also preceded by a hot spring, the effects on the entire countryside are there for all to see. Milder yet wetter winters with accompanying destructive storms appear to be part of the overall pattern. The use of drought-tolerant and xerophytic plants and gravel gardens, together with water-absorbing plantings and swales, will become an integral part of environmental management, landscape architecture and garden design. The garden and the landscape of the future will look entirely different.

John Edmiston, Director of Tropical Britain

Upcycled Materials and Structures

The idea of reusing or repurposing existing materials is not new. If one looks at history it abounds with instances of people creating new from old – one such example is Glasnevin Botanic Gardens, Dublin. The gardens themselves contain glasshouses of both historical and architectural importance that were becoming difficult to maintain – these include the Teak House, Palm House (1884) and the Curvilinear Range (which was first designed and built by Richard Turner in 1848). All were restored – two using some contemporary ironwork from Kew Botanic Gardens in London and which later attracted the Europa Nostra award for excellence in Architectural Conservation. Therefore, it is recommended here that one must always look first to using sustainable restoration or repairing rather than buying new.

It must also be noted there are other methods one can follow and that it is not impossible to build your own structures on open ground using recycled materials. Taking into consideration safety precautions prior to any attempt, the easiest method is to build a low polytunnel or fruit cage using repurposed medium density polythene (MDPE) pipe and a sheet of shading plastic or 'Super Therm' (or similar) polythene plastic, which can be bought at horticultural retailers. This is using plastic materials – which outlive metal by a considerable timeframe, so when disposing of it at the end of its natural life, remember it is all recyclable at the correct facility.

Allotments are creative spaces based on ultra-low budgets and have long been used as experimental places to build interesting structures. One such use of recycled materials – and one that takes skill and care – is to build a glasshouse from windows that would otherwise be thrown into landfill. Most double-glazing companies will come across the old wooden-type of

The glasshouses at Glasnevin, Dublin are excellent examples of restoration utilizing contemporary ironwork from Kew.

RIGHT: These types of hooped tunnels offer excellent year-round protection for relatively low cost.

BELOW: A sketched schematic of a recycled window and first experimental result. Whilst aesthetically odd, it was sturdy and against the south-west-facing concrete wall was more than adequate for growing cucumbers and melons. The roof and some panels were PVC sheets. A side panel was plastic drinks bottles that acted well as ventilators.

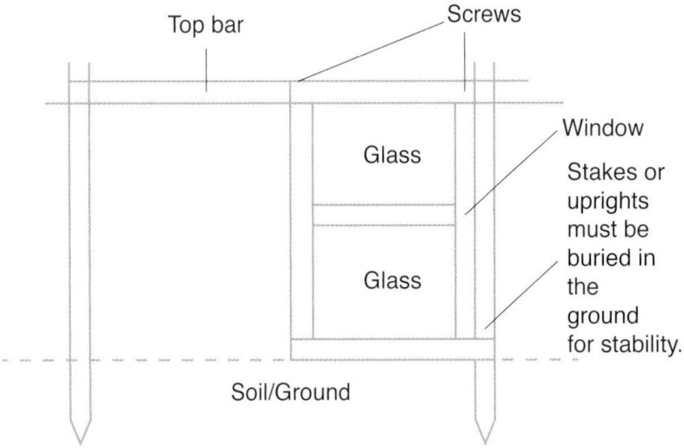

windows that were installed in houses up to the mid-twentieth century. They generally pay to have them recycled or, worst-case, dumped, therefore many will be willing for you to take them. Remember, this is not horticultural glass so will not give you the same results as a typical greenhouse; however, it will give you good results if used against a south- or west-facing wall, acting as a heat store. Due to the widely differing nature of the materials you will source, it is not within the capability of this book to precisely offer an accurate design for the project, therefore much latitude is to be expected in any build. However, you can follow loosely the following method. For the construction you will need:

- An accurate 5m tape-measure.
- Drill (make sure not to use anything electrical in wet conditions) with drill bit no bigger than the size of the screws you are using.
- Screwdriver.
- External screws long enough to go through the window frame and into the wooden frame behind to hold them in place (never use nails as the glass will probably shatter).
- Glazing putty.
- Beading and wood glue.
- Used sash windows acquired from a glazing company.
- Four 762mm x 762mm (or similar) treated wooden 2m stakes or fence posts.
- Treated 508 x 762mm wood to complete the frame.
- Metal hinges and fixing screws.
- Post hammer (if using stakes).
- Strong border spade.

As an additional measure, try to get windows that are the same or of similar size. This will help you in the next step of the build and reduce the chances of needing a complex frame – remember, the idea is to get as much sun as possible: the more wood used, the less surface area dedicated to glass. Make sure the glass is secure in the frame. Any loose glass can be secured in place by using beading and wood glue rather than nails.

Before you start, it is always good to have an idea of what shape your structure is going to take – a simple cube or rectangle with an angled flat roof (for drainage) is by far the easiest – a vernacular roof can be achieved, but the frontage will be over-complicated. Measure the windows you have acquired and put them together in order of similarity, then draw a rough plan using those measurements as a guide. At this stage, try to remove any ornamental features that make them odd shapes using a sharp saw – make them as square-edged as possible.

Once you have an idea of your design, you need to build a frame to fix your windows in place. It is by far the safest option to build a single-storey structure; therefore, for the frame you will need four stakes (or perhaps five depending on length) or fence posts fixed in place at each corner. The frame should have a top bar, which is used to affix the window-frames and also to support the top glass, so it should be of a decent strength to take the weight.

Once you are satisfied that the frame is secure and does not move, then you must set about affixing the windows to the frame by using screws as described – it is important for safety that you use several fixing

Be Warned

There are safety concerns and the following steps must be taken:

- Always handle glass products with thick gloves and safety glasses, taking great care.
- Check the frame. Many old wooden windows have issues with rot. If there is any rot in the wood, it will be a hazard for you or any users. If they are stable, but the paint is in a poor state, this can be rectified with the addition of exterior paint once the frame is cleaned.
- Check the glass. Cracks and breaks are an issue as they will degrade during cold spells causing a danger to users.
- When using tools, always make sure you are using them correctly and that you have the correct sturdy footwear and protective clothing.
- Check the putty or beading that is holding the glass in place. If this is damaged or loose, the glass can fall out, creating an additional hazard. This can be remedied by replacing the putty or installing new beading.

A pile of rubbish or a pile of materials awaiting reuse.

Ask an Expert

In your view, is there anything a gardener can do to increase sustainability on their (smaller scale) protective growing project?

The issue of sustainability is such a huge topic that many think their contribution to it needs to be large. However, many small changes can add up to a significant contribution. Materials to create covered structures can be kept as efficient as possible by maintenance. Washing of plastic tunnels and glass maximizes the amount of light the covered crops get. Cleanliness helps to maintain a healthy environment for crops and can minimize pests and diseases. Saving home seed, seed exchanges and sharing of excess seedlings helps keep us sustainable. Use of biodegradable potting containers when possible and using peat-free composts all help.

Brendan Sayers, Glasshouse Foreman,
National Botanic Gardens, Glasnevin, Ireland

points. It is far simpler to first drill holes through the window-frame and then simply screw directly into your support frame – rather than laboriously screwing into both window-frame and the structural frame. Remember, one window-frame will have to be used as a door. Before using the structure, make sure that all the glass is secure. If there is any looseness, use the glazing putty and allow to dry to finish.

The great advantage of experimenting with your own structure using sustainable methods is that you can utilize natural heating, such as in solar greenhouses.

What is the Provenance of the Materials Used in Your Project?

A question you should ask the seller (which is often overlooked): what is the provenance of the materials used? Most manufacturers should be aware if their raw materials were transported many thousands of miles from cheap factories – adding tonnes of carbon dioxide into the atmosphere – or made using forced labour (some companies offer guarantees that this has not happened). It is worth remembering, glass production in itself is highly inefficient when it comes to carbon dioxide output, so this is another consideration when buying new. If you wish to use other materials, the alternatives to glass are currently polycarbonate or acrylic – both of which utilize petroleum-based methods that (being plastic) degrade over time shedding micro-plastics into the ecology of the surrounding area and water supply, so always consider your choices carefully. That said, due to concerns with polycarbonate being toxic (when used in food containers), recent experiments have created a viable and safe product that also removes from the air and utilizes carbon dioxide in its structure – so your structure could be an effective carbon store and is worth researching before you purchase anything.

An exciting alternative is clear ceramic – which is still in the early stages of product development, but available. Utilizing aluminium compounds, such as magnesium aluminate or aluminium oxinitride, these manufactured products are being talked about for future space exploration and habitat creation – being reasonably low cost and easily sourced from available

This small area has been designed to offer a protective screen from harsh winds. MDPE piping is a most useful and recyclable product.

'Half cloches' saved from the skip, protecting early sown crops.

materials on the observed moons and planets space exploration is likely to visit in the near future, saving on expensive transportation from Earth.

Encouraging Biodiversity

An interesting concept first thought of in the twentieth century, but gaining traction in the twenty-first, is to plant a skirt of wildflowers around the greenhouse. Of course, if your garden is well maintained and floriferous, this will not be an issue. However, it has become a habit for many garden owners – who are time-poor – to ask for a garden of 'low maintenance'. This invariably leads to mass planting of similar evergreen shrubs that require little input but a trim – which aesthetically can be pleasing, but to our vital insects offers a desert. Accordingly, as discussed elsewhere in this book, it is always better to plant a hedge with wildlife in mind. What one may assume to be a pest, may also be a pollinator or a vital food source for beneficial birds and garden predators.

A wildflower meadow next to the newly built greenhouse. The skirt needn't be extensive, but will encourage biodiversity.

Ask an Expert

Are there any tips for encouraging biodiversity?

Once you have a hedge, cutting every year (after the nesting season, so well after August) can remove the berries before they get to set and provide food for wildlife, and potentially you'll also cut the stems that would have the flowering buds for the following year. Ideally a hedge cut might be carried out every other year. Even better, if this cut could be done in some kind of alternating way: maybe one side and the top one year, and the other side the next, or a stretch one year and the following stretch another. Then you can make sure there are always berries and flower buds available for spring and some thicker cover for overwintering roosting birds.

Rory Harding, Farmer Cluster Officer,
Kent Wildlife Trust

A hand-made glasshouse. Aesthetically pleasing and viable, this glasshouse was made by Aaron Harris, an English teacher utilizing YouTube tutorials and with no formal training in woodworking.

A simple cloche of fleece protects these peas from bird attack and the scorching rays of the sun. This approach also works for frosts but may not work for all plants, especially young seedlings.

*Make sure any fabric purchased has enough excess at either end and sides of the cloche.

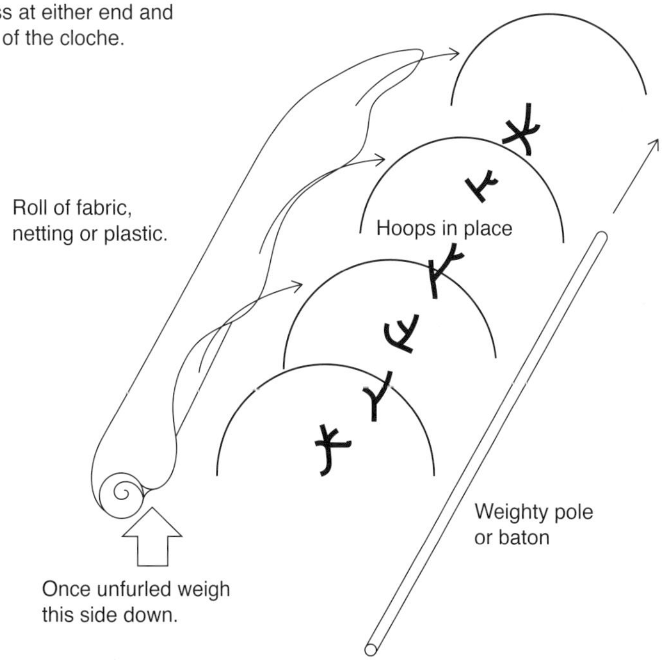

1. Place your MDPE hoops in the required position.
2. Unroll the fabric over the hoops, keeping enough fabric at each end to seal them.
3. Weigh down on one side with bricks or dig in with soil.
   The other side, tighten the slack by rolling excess on to a weighty baton.
4. Tie up excess ar both ends with twine or cable ties to seal.
5. To allow air movement during hot spells, lift weighted baton and support with bricks.

How to make a sustainable protective cloche, using no nails or other wastage of materials.

A Viable Alternative to Weedkiller

For information on herbicides and pesticides, *see* Chapter 9. A viable alternative, other than hand-weeding, is plant electrocution. A relatively new concept, trials have proved successful and it is now in the mainstream. The concept is simple: an electrode connected either to the mains or a generator (*importantly* with the machine and the trained operator being earthed), the natural resistance of the plant acts to destroy it by conducting the electricity into areas that contain water or liquids. This liquid is evaporated, thus destroying cell membranes and the plant dies. According to a study by John Reed of Silsoe Technology Ltd in 2009:

> Electrical weeding offers a number of advantages over conventional methods, e.g. timeliness (could work after rain and in bad soil conditions when hoes would be inappropriate), does not disturb soil, lower cost than hand-weeding, no toxic residue, no soil retention issues, not wind affected.... The financial benefits of electrical weeding to the industry would accrue as a result of the technique being available as an alternative to herbicide, hand or mechanical treatments.

There are some downsides to this that should be considered:

- Younger weeds are more likely to be killed than older specimens.
- Single-stemmed weeds are generally easier to control than many-branched weeds.
- Several applications may be required to fully eradicate the problem from an area.
- Conductivity can be unreliable in large areas, so it is best suited to areas with low weed density.
- Electrical equipment should not be used in areas of high water presence or in wet weather.

Remember

Electricity is dangerous and can cause death or serious injury. Training and correct safety procedures should always be followed.

- Tests show that using electricity is 'five times slower than chemical control and requires twice the energy' (from the study: *Electrical Weed Control in Field Vegetables*. John Reed, Silsoe Technology Ltd (2009)).

All that said, in areas where weed control is important but the use of herbicides is not an option – such as wildlife-sensitive areas or organic farms – this is a very useful tool to have in the armoury.

The Water Conundrum

It is one of the most vital resources, yet water is one of the most overlooked resources. It is imperative that strict water regime be instigated in the garden in order to conserve a rare resource. Follow these guidelines to reduce water loss:

- Water in the evenings when evaporation risk is lower.
- Use waste water from the local domestic supply before using fresh water, if possible (especially when damping down in the greenhouse).
- Try to use watering systems that use less water.
- Water heavily – less frequently – making sure the soil is saturated, rather than a small amount often.

A simple and sustainable idea utilizing both hydroponics and recycling has been created by Bottle Farm Ltd. By following the carefully written instructions provided in the kit, you can create a growing environment utilizing plastic water bottles that mimic vertical indoor farms.

Ask an Expert

How do you recycle water or do you mitigate against water waste?

We had major restorations of glasshouse complexes between 1995 and 2005 and as part of the projects, rainwater harvesting was incorporated by using large, underground, rainwater tanks. Although exempt, when hosepipe bans are in place for the country or capital, we limit outdoor watering and only water with watering cans. On glasshouses that are not connected to the harvesting system, large water-butts collect rainwater.

Brendan Sayers, Glasshouse Foreman,
Botanic Gardens, Glasnevin, Ireland

- Keep an eye on the weather. If it is set to rain, wait until after the event and assess its usefulness to the plants.
- Try to reduce water wastage by turning off taps when not needed. Make sure leaks are dealt with and prevented from happening (insulate pipes against frosts). Cover water-storage butts or tanks to reduce evaporation.
- Use mulch to reduce evaporation and aid soil structure.

So, what are the alternatives?

- **Installation of water butts:** A simple method that takes advantage of rain. However, future climate models suggest arid regions, so this may be a short-term solution.
- **Borehole:** Currently unregulated. An expensive option that utilizes underground water reserves. However, as water shortages become more acute, this alternative will no doubt become licensed.
- **Catchment ponds:** A simple option but with land costs high, currently unfavourable. As problem species, such as disease-bearing mosquitoes, migrate north, these ponds would have to be monitored closely, but are not unviable.
- **Removal from rivers:** The most controversial of all the alternatives. If you are lucky enough to have a garden abutting a river or stream, you will need a licence from the water authority and environment agency to draw any amount of water from it. A limited resource: according to a study carried out by the World Wildlife Fund in 2017, a staggering 24 per cent of UK rivers are in danger of permanently running dry.

The Solar Greenhouse

An idea first experimented with in northern China and now highly popular – providing fresh vegetables throughout the harsh Chinese winter. The costs are relatively low, as the equipment needed is simple and easily acquired. The basic principle is to utilize the energy of the sun to heat a bank of earth or a wall, so that it is released over time to keep the temperature of the greenhouse constant. It also has the advantage of having absolutely no input from costly electrical or gas-powered heating systems (*see* Chapter 5). During the day, the wall acts in an endothermic way, trapping heat; during the night, it becomes exothermic, releasing the energy in a remarkably steady way. The design is based on three separate units: the heat-retaining wall, a rear roof and a front roof.

One example of a useable solar greenhouse was owned and built by Peter Howell in 1975. Located at an altitude of 2,500m above sea level, the local meteorological conditions were extreme. Using steel-framed arches from a Nissen-style hut, the structure was covered with two layers of 10mm opaque vinyl. A dead air-space of 100mm was left between the two layers to provide the insulation layer. Blackened 55 gallon oil drums, filled with water, were installed. These had the primary aim of absorbing the sun's heat during the day and then losing it at night – acting as storage heaters and preventing drastic temperature changes. Crops such as lettuce and peas were grown all winter. In May,

Heating a solar greenhouse needn't be as complex as in some experiments using large barrels (or using drinks cans, *right*). The principle is stacking the aquifers, like plastic milk containers painted with inexpensive black paint (*left*), in direct sunlight and insulating them to retain heat.

The solar greenhouse of Peter Howell located at 8,500ft above sea level.

with a foot of snow and a temperature of 1°C outside the structure, it was 26°C inside.

Growing Food Indoors

As this book has endeavoured to show, the idea that people can grow their own fresh food in a protective environment is not new. However, a relatively recent exploration on the theme is food production that seeks to explore environments with no external contamination and minimal waste.

It has been common for many of us to grow herbs on a warm windowsill, but technology has advanced to the stage that indoor vegetable-growing systems are now very much a viable alternative for those with limited space. Mostly utilizing hydroponics (*see* Chapter 3), the microcomputer systems regulate light, temperatures and nutrient supply in a simple to use way, making the reality of fresh food available to all.

On a larger scale, carefully controlled computer-led vertical systems are being successfully used in urban farms to supply restaurants (*see* Chapter 4). Because the idea is specifically designed to be utilized in any space, the restrictions of light and temperature means food can be grown in a basement or other area with no access to the sun, such as a shipping container. Being a 'controlled environment agriculture platform', it utilizes

Staging in the growing space needn't be expensive. These were made using rough-cut wood and pallets. Easily cleaned, they can be moved without difficulty.

soilless agriculture technologies developed by NASA called aeroponics (*see* Chapter 3). LED lighting, installed to the correct specifications for the plants being grown (*see* Chapter 4), provides a low-cost (and low-heat) source of energy. A further technological innovation is the use of sensors that monitor the climate within the specialized growing chamber, adjusting it as and when needed to remain at optimum growing conditions. The great strides forward with this technology have meant that upsizing has proved no difficulty.

CHAPTER 7

HEALTH AND HYGIENE

> 'Hygiene, physical culture will be recognized branches of education and government. The Secretary of Hygiene or Physical Culture will be far more important in the cabinet of the President of the United States who holds office than the Secretary of War ... Our water supply will be far more carefully supervised, and only a lunatic will drink unsterilized water.'
>
> Nikola Tesla, *Liberty Magazine* (1935)

The premise that prevention is better than cure is something that all gardeners should take to their hearts. All gardens are a contrivance. What the grower has actively sought to achieve in aesthetics or practicality – by placing row upon row of the same or similar plants together in a confined space – they have provided the perfect space for whatever pathogen those plants fear most. However, because the environment has been built, it can also be controlled. A most important role for any gardener or grower is to make sure the closed microclimate they have constructed is as close to 'healthy' as possible. To practise cleanliness is to save a lot of work later on.

Constant vigilance is key; spotting the first signs of plant stress (through attack by pests or disease to lack of water or too much/too little heat) is essential. Rubbish and any other odd items, such as clippings, spent soil or compost, dirty plant-supports, uncleaned or unused seed trays, should never be stored in the greenhouse. Have no doubt, they will harbour the very things you are trying to remove from the environment. Be aware that creating a monoculture can be just as hazardous. According to research done by Julia Anderson, Emily Hespeler and Steven Zwiren at the Univerity of Massachusetts, the form of horticulture that pushes one crop can have poor results:

> Despite high yields and relatively low input prices, growing just one species of crop on many acres of land creates major pest problems.... Overcrowding genetically uniform plants allows pests to spread through fields with relatively little resistance, compared to a more diverse array of species.

Further, the authors of the university blog note:

> The inherent issues of pest management in monoculture systems will be exacerbated by the effects of climate change. Increases in average temperature creates a favorable environment that support larger pest populations. All insects are cold-blooded organisms, meaning that their body temperatures and biological processes directly correlate to environmental temperatures (Petzoldt & Seaman, 2006; Bale & Hayward, 2010) .... Warmer temperatures increase pest populations and

Mealy bugs are a nuisance as they attack plants, sucking their sap and exuding a 'frass' that protects them. Once an infestation starts, it is very difficult to eradicate them, as they hide in old pots, cracks in walls, etc.

decrease the efficacy of pesticides. Furthermore, overuse of pesticides is allowing pests to develop pesticide resistance, creating a snowball effect between pests, pesticide usage, and pesticide resistance.

Best Practice for Hedges and Screens

If you are inspecting a hedge, keep an eye on the bark or branches. Many pest species, such as woolly aphid, overwinter in hedges. Lightly feed the hedge in early spring with a blood, fish and bone preparation to ensure healthy growth. Remove pests by hand if at all possible; otherwise spray with the safest horticultural oil available – carefully following the health and safety guidelines printed on the label. Fences and walls should be inspected carefully for damage (making sure 'damage' is not the result of solitary bees creating nests). Broken pointing, cracks and other areas where pests may congregate need to be addressed – bearing in mind helpful insects, such as ladybirds, will mass hibernate in the same spaces. Rotten wooden supports can be food for soil-borne fungus, so need replacing. Effective weed management is also key. Some pathogens will easily transfer to other species.

> Some pathogens also need to find alternative hosts when a fruit host is unavailable. For example, the root knot nematode can also reproduce on dandelions in vineyards. This weed can also serve as a host for viruses that are vectored by the dagger nematode. Weed management is essential to reduce these types of risk. Cover crops that suppress weeds and nematodes have been used in fruit systems and are likely to play an even more important role in the future.
>
> (*Fruit Crop Ecology and Management* (2002), Larry Gut, Annemiek Schilder, Rufus Isaacs and Patricia McManus at Michigan State University)

Best Practice in an Enclosed Growing Environment

According to the University of Massachusetts at Amherst, it is favourable to disinfect the greenhouse between crop cycles, especially early in the season, to remove pests that may have overwintered. Make sure that the disinfectant is suitable (and legally approved) for the job you are using it. If in doubt, check either the www.soilassociaton.org or www.omri.org for further guidance, as their information will be updated in accordance with government regulations. Make a point of looking in corners and under staging. Start at

An unclean greenhouse is something that many are guilty of without realizing it. Old pots filled with spent soil, old plant materials, plastic ties and other garden ephemera can harbour pests and should be stored in a shed.

Ask an Expert

Are there any simple tips you can share for basic continued plant health?

It's vital to create the right environment for the chosen plants to grow in, if plants are grown in appropriate environments they will be strong and healthy and able to ward off many P&D issues. Grow a variety of plants, as they will be less susceptible to P&D spread, maintain good air movement and growing conditions, encourage biological life and presence of beneficial insects and be observant, as it's much easier to treat P&D when they first appear than after they have established.

Scott Taylor, Conservatories Manager,
Kew Botanic Gardens

the top of the space, scrubbing with a brush and working your way down to the floor. Pathogens and vectors will find nooks in which to form a colony. Pick up any detritus and dispose of plant waste or organic matter, making sure that the area is clean of wastage. Check and replace any matting with signs of algae infestation. Weed carefully and thoroughly. Irrigation systems should be cleaned through using a specific treatment.

Set up a cleaning station near the entrance. Wash your hands and boots if walking from the garden borders directly into an enclosed space. This is most important around the propagation area where plants are most susceptible to infection.

During the growing season, a gardener's best practice is to inspect crops or plants on a daily basis for any signs of attack so that they can be managed immediately. If you are time-poor or if the space is too large to manage on limited staff numbers, artificial intelligence such as Phytlsigns can be installed that will check for plant stress, pest and diseases and irrigation or watering problems via the biological processes known as electrophysiology.

Use approved horticultural oils (such as neem or rapeseed) on vegetation near the greenhouse to reduce the likelihood of pests entering.

It is only possible to obtain reasonable yields by growing in a healthy growing medium. Many books stipulate that in the greenhouse it is vital that the soil is refreshed by the introduction of new sterilized medium every growing season – the main aim is to *prevent*.

Remember: once a possible infestation has become established, it will cost you time and money.

If you are an amateur, keep in mind the principle that within a closed environment, the soil will quickly be spent of nutrients and that soil toxins will build up over a relatively short time. No addition of a chemical-based fertilizer can replace the structure that is needed for your plant's well-being. Look to remove and replace

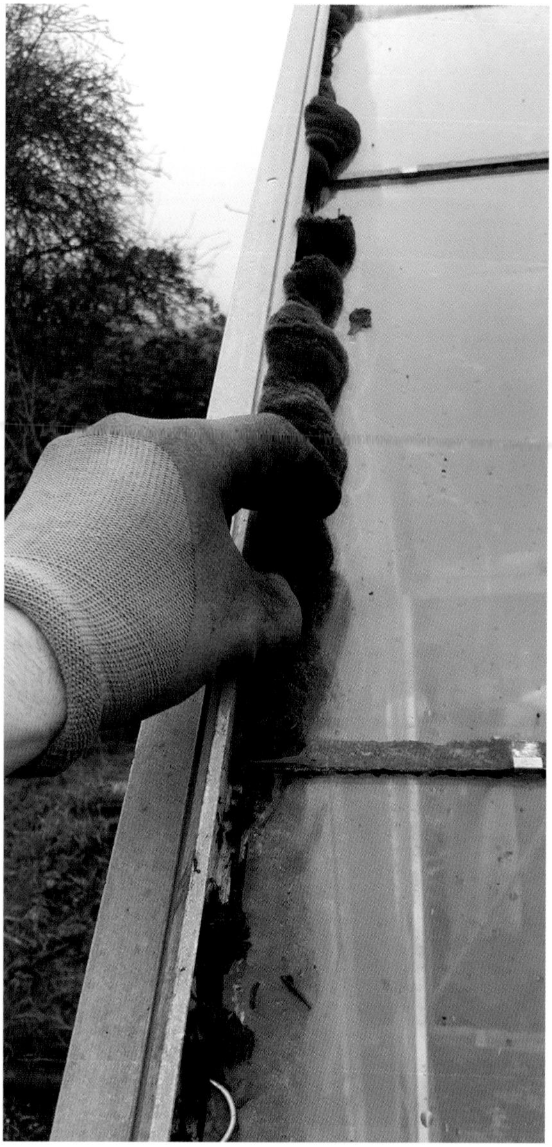

Rotting wood can harbour many problems from insects to fungi, so needs fixing or replacing.

Remember

Cleaning a house will reduce and remove pathogens but will not prevent them from being reintroduced. Make sure to clean areas thoroughly where roots have been in contact with staging surfaces (especially wood, which can harbour algae) or brickwork. Also make sure the floor does not pool water and that it drains well.

ABOVE LEFT: Part of a gardener's job is to inspect the growing space. This includes checking glass, the state of the wood or metal, checking for pest and disease and abnormal growth, such as moss or algae, which will reduce light levels.

Protection from frost is vitally important, so too is keeping equipment in top condition.

your growing medium on an affordable cycle to suit your pocket. Alternatively, if you cannot do this, it is better to stand pots or other containers of compost on the borders and grow your crops in these – it is not unheard of to bury these containers in the ground to preserve the aesthetic, lifting them at the end of the growing season for hygiene reasons. If your growing frame is light enough, perhaps think about moving it to a new site in the garden every few years to allow the area to readjust and rebalance.

Ask an Expert

In commercial glasshouse production, what are the major do's and dont's?

Ventilation is a big issue. Our greenhouse was put up in the 1980s and is getting a little old. Trying to update it is a challenge. Keep on top of pest and disease in the glasshouse. Get to know your glasshouse where you have areas that dry out more than others and knowing your crops in the glasshouse like-wise – what needs different microclimates and watering.

Helen Howard, Managing Director, Howard Nursery

Health and Safety

Your health and wellbeing must be included in your approach to gardening: According to the Royal Society for the Prevention of Accidents, it is estimated that 87,000 people are injured in UK gardens each year, some of which are the result of reactions to chemicals. From a basic perspective, being careful and considerate, wearing the correct clothing and using appropriate equipment are vitally important in all circumstances. According to the Institute for Environmental Health at Leicester University (1997):

> The enclosed conditions mean that greenhouse workers are more likely to be exposed to higher levels of plant material, plant pests and plant protection products than general horticulture workers.... The principal potential effects expected include irritancy, asthma, allergic aleveolitis and dermatitis.

Also within the study, to a lesser extent there was some incidence of non-Hodgkin's lymphoma (from misuse of chemicals), lower sperm counts and long-term respiratory disease in greenhouse workers that used chemical controls. Recurring contact with the same pest and disease can lead to problems with dermatitis and respiratory problems – a common complaint is reaction to plant materials such as chrysanthemum, tulip or lettuce. The reaction to pathogens such as fungi that commonly occur is a further concern.

Falling glass is a very serious hazard. Replace putty as soon as it becomes brittle.

The Discipline of Buying Your Plants and Seeds from Good Sources

A major step forward for all growers is the 'International Seed Health Initiative', which promotes the need for clean seeds globally. Chemical companies, such as Bayer, have been introducing ideas such as their 'SHIELD' programme, which is committed to providing clean seeds, season after season to all food producers – as part of their 'Health for All, Hunger for None' approach. Undermining this approach are the freely available seeds that one can buy or swap online. It is imperative that all seeds and plant material introduced into your garden are of the best quality and from a trusted supplier. Whilst it is tempting to seek out a rarity or a bargain, the introduction of new, unknown pathogens can not only devastate your garden, but if released into the wider environment, will have serious environmental impacts.

Green Bridges

A simple premise: if plants are placed too close together, a 'green bridge' is created. Whilst it is certainly not possible within the wider garden to keep plants individually apart, following the correct husbandry methods and remembering the 'three D's' of pruning, removing the dead, diseased and damaged, helps. Within the greenhouse, the potager and allotment, there is a more pressing need to keep plants separated because of the very real possibility of cross-contamination. As with all plantings that consist of the same variety or species, there is a heightened risk of a pathogen marching through the space unhindered. It is prudent of the grower to keep his or her tools clean, to inspect regularly and to follow a clear path. Within a protective hedge scenario, this routine is virtually impossible – saving making sure that the plants are well watered and well cared for with any opportunity for a pest or fungus to infest reduced to a minimum. If any disease is spotted, remedial action must be undertaken at the earliest opportunity.

Fumigation

Fumigants are primarily used for phytosanitary purposes in the greenhouse or polytunnel to treat diseases that are otherwise untreatable by other methods. They can be bought from most specialist garden retailers or ordered online from approved suppliers.

NB Be sure to buy from reputable sources, as counterfeiting is prevalent and will result in inadvertent poisoning; be sure to wear the correct PPE when handling. Also, according to the The International Plant Protection Convention, there are strict guidelines that must be followed if you are intending to use fumigation in order to treat imported plants or are doing so before export. More can be read on the ippc.int website.

On the smaller domestic scale, the downside to fumigation is that the glasshouse or tunnel atmosphere for some time afterwards becomes awash with a chemical that is not good to inhale. Check too that the

In a spanned-roof greenhouse or polytunnel, the length (A–B) the breadth (C–D) and the height (B–E), (to halfway up the roof slope) should be multiplied together. If all the measurements are taken in millimetres, a further simple conversion will give the volume of the house in cubic metres.

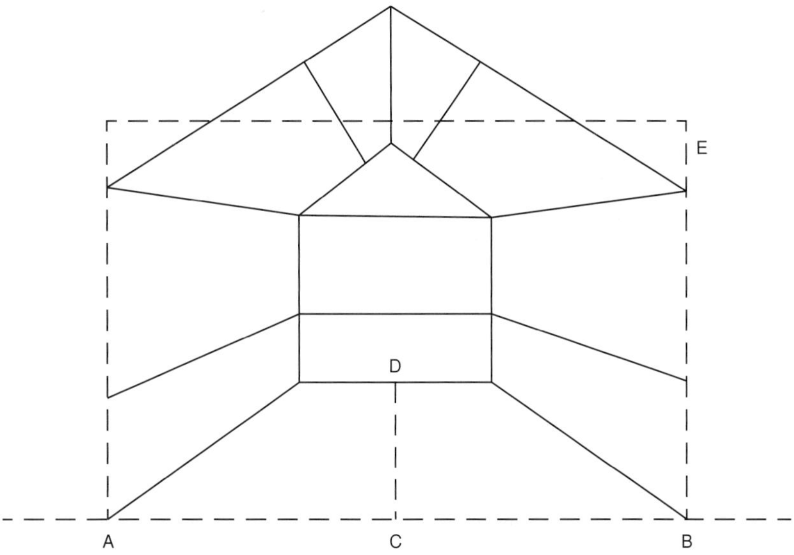

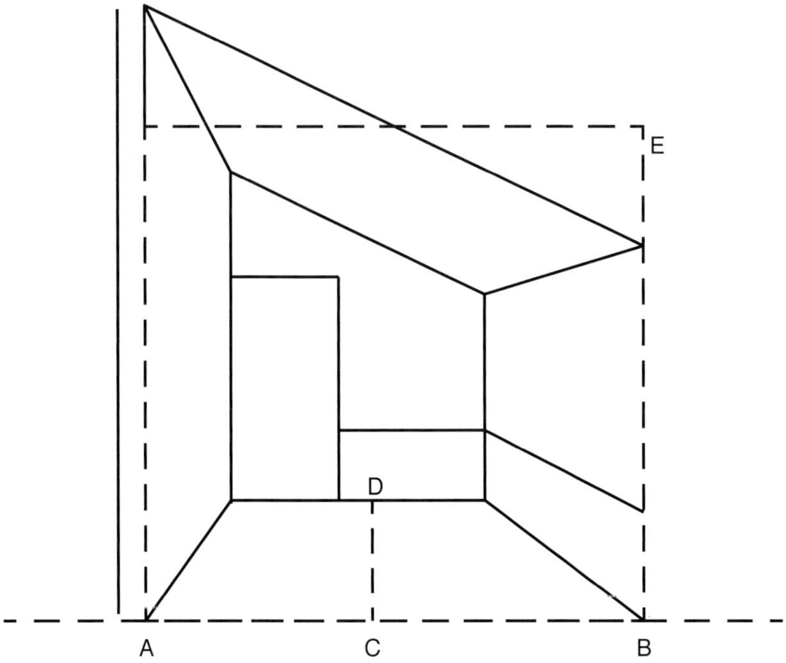

In a lean-to house the same approach is made using the previous formula.

plants concerned will not react adversely to the chemical used.

First, if you have the measurements to hand via the original schematic drawings, work out the cubic capacity of air within the space you are intending to treat. If not, measure your space using the guidance plan provided. Once this is done, follow the instructions on the packet provided by the manufacturer carefully to avoid accidents or to inadvertently negate the full effect required to eradicate the pest.

Before using the fumigator, the greenhouse or space should be made as airtight as possible. Use wet cloths or sacking to stop any gaps or cracks, if they are found. Close and lock all ventilation. You should not fumigate when temperatures are above 21°C (70°F), or when the house is in bright sunshine, as you may damage the plants. The best time to fumigate is in the evening but not too late that you cannot make sure the process is complete. Once you are satisfied that the process is finished, close the greenhouse or growing space and ventilate it well the following morning.

The Importance of Keeping Your Tools and Surfaces Clean

It would be unconscionable for a surgeon to operate on a patient without first checking that they *and* their tools were clean, yet, garden tools such a pruning knives, secateurs and shears are used and reused without a second thought to the disease they might harbour. For example, the two fungi known as 'box blight' (*Cylindrocladium buxicola* or *Volutella buxi*) are easily carried on shears from garden to garden, surviving on the blades for several months, perhaps years. If the garden you have created has heavily used the plant *Buxus sempervirens*, this will have devastating consequences. A simple cleanse of tools using Jeyes fluid or dilute bleach is usually effective (due to the nature of cell structures, alcohol cleaners should be *no more* or *no less* than 70 per cent strength). Making sure that the same clothes are never worn twice in infected areas without washing them first can also reduce risk – so too checking and disinfecting the soles of gardening boots.

In areas where conditions are constantly at a premium for disease to spread – such as in heated glasshouses – every gardener should have a small sterilization spray to hand to disinfect tools after *every* plant. This regime can be extended to digging tools, such as forks, trowels and spades, if the gardener believes it is warranted. A further regime must be followed when using and reusing pots, containers and seed trays. Many diseases can lie dormant on surfaces for days, weeks, months and even years – awaiting the ideal conditions to germinate and recolonize.

Keep to strict hygiene standards throughout the year to minimize cross-contamination. To wait until the end of the 'unofficial' growing season – generally December or January – to deep-cleanse tools and working area, is a mistake; climate models suggest it is prudent to adjust this habit to a rolling system. Clean and store pots as you go, rather than waiting for them to build into a job lot. (From an ecological point of view it is far better to reuse planters than to constantly buy new, but this comes with responsibilities.) Sweep the greenhouse paths regularly – making sure to remove anything that may harbour a disease. Scrub down hard surfaces with a soap solution every few months if possible. Change gravel or other drainage mediums for fresh – this needn't be thrown away, merely deep cleaned in another area for future use if possible.

It has been noticed in some commercial growing spaces that weed seeds are a constant presence, so a street sweeper has been employed to reduce the burden on time and labour. On a small-scale operation this method is not possible, but it is worth investing in a dustpan and brush or hand-held vacuum cleaner if this is an issue.

Finally, scrub the inside and outside of the glasshouse or polytunnel (including beams and bars) on a regular basis with a dilute cleaning solution. Not only will this hamper the build-up of algae – preventing vital light from entering – it also pre-empts spores or micro-organisms from finding safe harbour.

Keeping Your Plants Healthy

In order to tackle this subject properly, we have to take specific approaches according to what you are trying to achieve. Obviously the introduction of plants to any new environment causes a certain amount of stress – not only to the plant but to the already established flora and fauna. Therefore, it is wise to assume that a

Watering badly can cause unwitting hazards. Salt build-up on leaves can create scorch and encourage pests. In enclosed environments, try to water at the roots, not the leaves.

healthy, protective screen needs a slightly different care regime from a line of celtuce growing in a poly-tunnel. Always feed the soil (and therefore the plant) at the correct times, making sure it is not waterlogged. Understand your plant and its needs – it may need higher humidity, drought or darkness.

Excess Fertilizer and Water is as Damaging as No Food and Water!

The factor of over-watering and over-feeding is an interesting and important anomaly, often overlooked in many garden books. Over-watering leads to wilting. Quite reasonably, the grower is led to the mistaken belief that the plant needs water, leading to a pattern of behaviour exasperating the situation.

Yellow leaves falling is also a classic sign that things are not well in the soil. This is often caused by the cells becoming damaged, or by root-rot. A simple test is to always check the soil before watering, if it is mildly damp it will not need watering. Also, it is key that you understand your plants. Many houseplants need a rest period in winter or early spring – their natural environment could be going through the 'dry season'. This is a time when watering should be reduced to a minimum.

'Over-feeding' leads to symptoms that at first you may miss: yellowing of leaves, slow to no growth, browning of leaf margins. The soil will sometimes show signs of too many minerals present – especially in closed environments or pots – by developing a crunchy

Some diseases are made worse by genetic susceptibility, so choose varieties carefully. Hygiene in such instances is key, remembering to clear any detritus and that the cleaning of tools is essential. Black spot (a fungus called *Diplocarpon rosae*) affects roses, which have the recessive gene weakness in their lineage. Treating it with fungicide resolves the issue in the short term but, ultimately, leads to fungicide resistance and in the long-term the problem gets worse as the fungus adapts.

Ask an Expert

How do you keep heat and humidity satisfactory without encouraging devastating pathogens such as fungi?

Ventilating at the most appropriate time of day helps keep a buoyant and fresh atmosphere under cover. During winter a house may only be ventilated for a few hours, but this will be done when the daily temperatures are at their highest. Where composts in beds and pots are wet, humidity levels can be kept high by watering hard surfaces only, which will keep water away from plants and help against plant pathogens. Winter temperatures under cover are lowered and a balancing lowering of the amount of water given will also assist in not creating negative conditions for plants while their metabolism is at low levels.

Brendan Sayers, Glasshouse Foreman,
National Botanic Gardens, Glasnevin, Ireland

Remember

The basis of many chemical herbicides actively encourages the plant to overgrow to the point of collapse – it literally exhausts itself.

white crust. The first rule of feeding a plant is to understand that fertilizer is *not* plant food. It makes available materials the plant needs in order to grow well, so do not assume that you are giving your plants a slap-up meal every time. If these minerals (or just some) are too abundant, the plant cannot utilize them. Not only that, the fertilizer or soil sweetener (excess calcium) can prevent other vital processes from happening, such as the uptake of water or uptake of iron. It is always worthwhile getting a thorough soil test done on a yearly basis in order to understand what is missing and what is in abundance, then add fertilizer accordingly.

NB The following observations in table form are somewhat arbitrary as plants do not all act in the same way, however it will give you an idea of what to look for.

Further Limiting Factors

Protective Hedge

To disturb the existing microclimate by the introduction of a new protective hedge-line is something many gardeners don't take into consideration. Of course it is installed with the intention of creating a new, protected environment, with little consideration as to what went before. Ask yourself the following questions: Will the plants thrive in the situation provided? What was *in situ* before you planted the new hedge? (A previous conifer hedge will have robbed the soil of major nutrients or old tree stumps may have been a safe harbour for disease.) Do you need to provide a temporary shelter in the form of a windbreak or fence whilst the new plants establish? Do I have to remove the old soil or simply add organic matter or humus to improve it (using calculations in Chapter 3, or following the rule of one very full barrow per $8m^2$)? Am I planting at the right time? Am I creating a good climate or introducing more problems by stifling the airflow, introducing shade or creating a frost pocket?

The Closed Environment

Whether you are planning to use a small home-made cold-frame or a much larger structure, you are creating a false environment. All greenhouse books (that cover plants in any detail, no matter their skill level) will cover the various climates and conditions needed for specific genres. It is pertinent to seek out specific books for the type of plant that you are interested in before you invest in a greenhouse – a stove house cannot be built, with any success, using a small aluminium domestic frame that you inherited when you bought the property or found on Freecycle. The commercial grower has a far greater problem, in that they must consider the needs of specific plants *en masse* – whilst houseplants can put up with a multitude of domestic situations, it is key that they are at their best when prepared for the marketplace. The same goes for vegetables or fruit. In this way, a commercial grower's main concern is wastage rather than longevity.

For the amateur, once you have researched thoroughly alpine growing or orchid growing, or whatever it is you are aiming to do with your space, you should consider your best options: have you costed every-

Table 5 Signs of mineral deficiencies or excesses

Aluminium	Excesses occur in very acid soils, when insoluble aluminium becomes soluble. Symptoms include damping-off of some seedlings, coupled with lack of root hairs.
Ammonia	Caused most often by overuse of fresh manures. Symptoms of excess are: very soft growth, with dark green blotches as if damaged by wind or frost.
Boron	Can affect different plants in different ways. In tomatoes, leaves can be highly coloured. In fruits, a sign of death of cells below the skin.
Calcium	Deficiencies arise in highly acid soils, which harms micro-organisms. Symptoms of deficiency are poor growth, sour soil, shoot dieback. Symptoms of excess are iron deficiency and chlorosis in lime-hating plants.
Copper	Quite a rare deficiency, sometimes can be a poison in industrial areas. Symptoms of deficiency are especially present on apples and pears with dieback of branches and bark diseases. Symptoms of excess are blue and black mottling on stems of seedlings.
Iron	Present in most soils except highly calcified. Symptoms of deficiency are chlorosis – the yellowing of leaves (not stems). Excesses are very rare as it becomes 'locked'.
Magnesium	Shortages most likely to occur in sandy or free-draining soils. Symptoms of deficiency are interveinal yellowing of lower leaves that gradually progresses up the plant, with reduced growth. Excess in soil will cause an 'insoluble salts build-up' that needs flushing as it will greatly restrict plant growth.
Manganese	Can be flushed out of soils by high rainfall. Deficiency symptoms are mottling and extreme wilting. Excesses will cause wither, droop and dead patches on leaves.
Molybdenum	A gas in the soil, deficiency is most evident in brassicas with a narrowing of leaves.
Nitrogen	Most likely deficient in lighter soils with low organic matter, locked in clay or highly organic marshy soils. Deficiency usually shows by smaller plants with yellow colour. Excess results in leggy plants with unproductive growth.
Oxygen	A gas. Lack of oxygen usually occurs in heavily flooded soils, or areas of compaction. Plants will show a yellowing of leaves and death without remedial action.
Potassium	A lack of potassium generally results in very soft growth with a browning of leaf edges in some plants. Excess can lead to a scorched appearance on leaf tips with excessive curling. The roots are generally shallower than they should be, creating issues for the plant's ability to take up food.
Zinc	Deficiency evident in apple orchards with smaller fruit with very narrow leaves. Excess can come from galvanized wire netting leaching into the soil and results in poor growth.

thing? (i.e. build costs, soil and compost costs, buying seeds versus buying plants, the costs of replacement due to wear and tear, cost in time, cost in labour, natural market inflation). Referring to Chapter 5, is it cost-effective in the short- *and* long-term to keep your house heated to between 18 and 21°C all year round? Referring to the discussion in Chapter 6, is your project sustainable? Do you have the time to keep your prized *Cattleya loddigesii* happy for 365 days a year?

Whilst none of these questions cover how to keep a specific plant happy, the stresses on your pocket or spare time will invariably aid any decisions on what you, the gardener, is actually capable of achieving. Thus, choices made early on will naturally lead to healthier plants and a happier gardener in the long run.

CHAPTER 8

PESTS AND DISEASE

'It is not about exploiting the weakness of your opponents, it's about realizing the aspects in which your opponents are strong and then controlling and managing them.'

Nuno Espirito Santo, Head Coach, Wolverhampton Wanderers FC (2020)

Signs of Pest and Disease Attack

Inspecting the Plant

A plant often causes concern when it 'looks' – to a human eye – abnormal. The problem may be immediately obvious – be it damage, wilting or discoloration, or the obvious presence of insects or fungus. These can all be discovered and dealt with during your everyday routine. However, symptoms can be more obtuse, only becoming evident via fastidious inspections by the more experienced gardener – sometimes indicating a more complex issue. Of course, insects can be vectors of disease too – an aphid bearing a viral infection or a beetle carrying a fungus. Therefore, it is up to the gardener to understand the specific threat cycles to foresee any issues. Remember, not all diseases are unintended – some plants, such as the contorted hazel (*Corylus avellana* 'Contorta'), are purposely infected to create the desired twisted stems, therefore one must prune out the straight-stemmed 'reversions' to keep the plant as it is intended.

Ask an Expert

Are there any tips for a glasshouse owner on how to minimize pests and disease?

Many! For a start, right plant for the right environment as this will limit P&D spread as the plant will grow healthily; plants get prone to P&D when under stress.

Good observation is also key, much easier to 'nip it in the bud' as in, remove P&D attacks when they first start, rather than once well-established when it becomes much more difficult.

Plant a variety of plants ... well suited to the environment created, as many different plants better suited to P&D resilience than if they are all the same. Good air movement, P&D thrive in stale air. Use and encourage beneficial insects including wasps, ladybirds, spiders etc.

Scott Taylor, Conservatories Manager, Kew Botanic Gardens

Botrytis on strawberries. Grown in close environments with little air movement and high humidity, fungi will ruin crops. Good hygiene includes removing any damaged or over-ripe fruit. Close inspection is always your first defence.

BELOW LEFT: The *Peziza* spp. fungus is sometimes a sign of disease in plant roots. Common on woodland floors, they inhabit hedges also.

Areas to inspect are: stems, roots, leaves, flowers and fruit (it is an idea to smell the surrounding soil too). These can all show symptoms of abnormal or poor growth, wilting, rotting, pest attack, discoloration or the subtle signs of fungal and bacterial infections. When the gardener senses something has gone wrong, they should try to discern why, so that they can enact remedial measures. Even where things have gone disastrously wrong and nothing can be done for the plant or, worse, the entire crop, steps must be taken to ensure the same does not happen to adjacent plants or future plantings.

That said, given the great strides modern humans have made in combating the grower's 'enemies' by the introduction of man-made chemicals, nature frequently fights back by genetically adapting.

For practical reference, Tables 6, 7 and 8 list some common pests and diseases and what to look out for (the list is not exhaustive).

Viral Diseases

Differing from bacteria in that they are not truly alive – borrowing some of their needed functions from the host cell and competing with the cell for vital food supplies – viruses are ancient in origin. The word virus means 'poison', which infers that they were discovered by the ancients. Instead the first discovery of viruses came in 1892 when two scientists studying a disease affecting tobacco plants discovered the new infectious agent – naming it tobacco mosaic virus. Since then it has been discovered that there are many more plant viruses than is generally now appreciated. Some plants are tolerant to some degree and may have built-up a resistance over time – sometimes causing an effect that becomes sought-after by plant collectors. Others are totally susceptible to infection and succumb quite quickly with a wide variety of symptoms.

It is quite common to find chemicals in sheds and greenhouses that are now illegal to use – or even store. Speak with the local council who will be able to help you dispose of them safely. Do not be tempted to use them and do not throw them away in the general waste – they could poison water supplies and many old pesticides are carcinogenic. *Go to* https://www.hse.gov.uk/pesticides/databases/index.htm for information.

Table 6 Common pests – invertebrates

Invertebrates	Animals with no vertebrae. These include insects, arachnids, molluscs and worms.
Aphids	Small, most often green or black, soft-bodied insects. Sometimes they have a protective woolly covering called 'frass' (*also see* mealy bugs). Can reproduce both asexually and sexually. Sap-sucking insects, they cause leaves to curl and pucker, stems weaken and droop. Their excretions can aid the growth of moulds. The plants can be sprayed with neem oil or rapeseed oil, which has some success. The introduction of predatory species, such as ladybirds and lacewings, is effective in their control within the greenhouse. Companion plants – such as *Calendula* – are suggested, but anecdotal evidence gives poor results and might actually encourage aphids.
Caterpillars	Wormlike creatures with short legs, they come in a variety of colours, some quite large. Leaving black specks of excrement on leaves, they eat and tear gaping holes in leaves. Left to their own devices they will consume an entire plant. Control often involves the laborious task of seeking them out by eye and removing them by hand. Prevention of flying parent from getting at the plants is quite often the most effective barrier and does not reduce local biodiveristy.
Cutworms	Largish, soft-bodied with wormlike bodies, they are actually surface-dwelling larvae of certain moths. They come out at night to eat irregular chunks out of leaves, working inwards from the margins. They are also responsible for eating through stems of young plants and seedlings. Hoeing regularly disturbs soil and exposes them to birds or similar predators.
Flatworms	Though not all are pests, introduced species are a serious pest. Encourage ground beetles, which are voracious predators. They are also attracted to lying at the surface under black plastic sheeting. If you know they are present in the garden, lay small traps in which you can collect and dispose of them humanely.
Leafminers	Invariably the larvae of various insects, they are small invertebrates that cause a distinctive 'mined' appearance on leaves, which appear speckled, may shrivel, turn yellow or brown or become blistered. Often speckled with excrement. Prevention is more often better than cure. Spraying the plant with neem oil is said to have some effect at reducing damage by putting the insect off. Pick off infected leaves once in evidence.
Mealy bugs	A pest under glass and in the house. A small insect, it produces a waxy frass that is incredibly difficult to eradicate. They overwinter in trees and hedges ready to cause havoc in spring. Pesticides are difficult to use due to the protective coating. Use neem oil or, if unavailable, rapeseed oil as a spray, which prevents them from breathing.

(*continued overleaf*)

Table 6 *continued*

Invertebrates	Animals with no vertebrae. These include insects, arachnids, molluscs and worms.
Nematodes	Microscopic creatures that live in the soil or are waterborne. Not all are necessarily bad for the garden – some attacking soil-borne pests such as keeled slugs or leatherjackets – and can be bought as Nemasys. Pest species cause roots to develop knots or galls, become shrunken or distorted. Once a plant is infected, chemical control is almost impossible, so prevention is better than cure. Growth ceases, leaves wilt and, if left unchecked, the plant dies. Use rapeseed as a green manure before planting – an active chemical in the plant is released as it breaks down, killing the nematodes. Use dahlia or French marigold as a companion plant to crops, as they both release chemicals via roots into the soil, which repels nematodes and eel worm.
Scale insects	Sap-sucking insects; some 8,000 different species exist. Brown discs appear under leaves or, more commonly, on stems. Leaves become mottled or spotted, fall off and die. Their excretions can aid the growth of moulds. Becoming more resistant to insecticides, treatment must be a considered approach. Neem oil is said to have some success at putting the insects off from attacking the plant in the first place. Biological predators include ladybirds and lacewings. If the infection is serious, systemic insecticides are available but becoming rarer. Under glass, fumigants can be used with caution and following correct procedures.
Slugs and snails	Molluscs. Recognizable either with the classic shell or their foot and 'saddle'. They leave a slimy trail as they travel, and chew rough holes through leaves and vulnerable stems. In the first instance it is best for the garden that predators are encouraged. Ground beetles, predatory slugs, birds and some small mammals favour slugs and snails as food. Predatory nematode washes can be bought easily and used under glass with no effect to the plants. Crushed seashells bought from a shellfish merchant and scattered throughout the border have a preventative effect. Beer traps have some use, but if dug too deep they have the adverse effect of trapping ground beetles and other predators. If all else fails, use slug pellets sparingly, being careful not to poison birds, predatory slugs or mammals (including pet dogs who will happily eat them).
Spider mites	Incredibly tiny members of the arachnid family, they are fast becoming resistant to chemical control. They spin coarse webbing across leaf axils and between leaves. An infested plant eventually turns yellow, its leaves mottled having grey or green splotches. Causes the plant to defoliate. The best method of control is through prevention. They adore warm, dry atmospheres under glass, so damping down to create a humid (but not stifling) atmosphere aids the cause. Wash walls with disinfectant.
Thrips	Can be notifiable, especially *Thrips palmi*, which is devastating to cucumber, tomato and sweet pepper production. Tiny needle-like insects that cause silver scarring, leaf deformation and chlorosis to leaves, flowers and fruit by sucking the contents from cells. Pockmarks or whitened surface most evident on underside of leaf. Flower buds drop off and leaves eventually develop a papery texture. Pruning the areas affected can reduce infection. Neem oil spray puts off insects from the plant. Use a gentle contact insecticide as a last resort, but resistance is increasing.
Whitefly	Small, moth-like pests. Cause leaves to yellow and wilt. Excreting a sticky substance that aids the growth of moulds. The introduction of parasitic wasps (*Encarsia formosa*) is the most economical way forward under glass; easily bought from stockists.

RIGHT: Black-fly and predators on a wildflower. If you must spray, make sure you are not killing an ally.

FAR RIGHT: Slugs and snails are a common pest throughout the warmer months. Remember, not all are pests.

FAR LEFT: Whitefly infesting a *Euonymus japonicus* hedge.

LEFT: A gall on a hedge-rose stem. Unsightly, they are result of damage by pest or accident. Prune them out if possible to prevent further infections.

Table 7 Common infections – fungal

Fungal infections	Fungi are a group of living organisms that have their own kingdom. They can be soil-borne or live within cells. They can, and will, attack living tissue if given the correct conditions. Difficult to eradicate, they are a growing concern in the garden as global temperatures increase.
Anthracnose	An infection, the chief characteristics of which are sunken spots (with dark rims and dry centres) on leaf surfaces. Leaf tips may shrivel and turn brown or be banded with darker stripes. Generally it attacks plants that have been chronically over-watered. Reduce watering to a bare minimum and remove all affected leaves.
Botrytis	A greyish-white growth that appears on soft-fruits (especially ripening strawberries and tomatoes) but also the upper leaves of plants such as African violets. It is highly contagious, so any fruit or plant should be removed as soon as first identified. Causes often include poor ventilation, plants too close together and watering habits that result in surfaces staying wet for prolonged periods. Try to give plants adequate space and ventilation (without increasing cold draughts).
Canker (fungal)	Most easily identified by open, weeping sores on the branches and trunk of trees and shrubs, it is difficult to discern whether the infection is fungal or bacterial. Fungal is often treatable, bacterial is often deadly. If the infection is in a branch, cleanly remove it using a saw. If the heart wood is very dark in colour, this means the infection is still in evidence. Remove more of the branch until no dark centre is in evidence. Feed the plant to aid recovery. If the canker is in the main trunk, then, depending on the severity of the infection, it may be best to remove the plant to prevent other nearby trees or plants from becoming infected.
Coral spot (*Nectria cinnabarina*)	A distinctive fungus often found on dead or dying wood affecting many trees and shrubs. Masses of tiny red or pink 'cushions' on branches, it can spread to healthy tissue causing dieback. Remove all affected wood via pruning, avoiding snags or untidy cuts. Do not let the infected wood lie about – either burn it for potash or dispose of it in the green waste collection.
Crown or stem rot	Caused primarily by bad husbandry – namely over-watering. Excessive humidity and either very high or very low temperatures all contribute to a variety of fungi attacking plants in a controlled environment. These fungi cause plant tissue along the stems and crown to rot, turning pulpy to the touch. If possible, cut out diseased parts, increase ventilation (without draught) and reduce watering to a bare minimum, remembering that most plants prefer a temperature of about 16°C.
Damping off	A fungal disease of untreated soil, it mainly affects seedlings. Occurring mostly in hot and humid conditions, it destroys young root and stem tissue; the plant will begin to bend, dying within a day of being infected. No plant should catch this if the soil has been pasteurized first.
Honey fungus (*Armillaria mellea*)	Known by many common names, this disease is incredibly destructive if left to get a foothold in a hedge-line. Primarily living on dead tree stumps and roots, it spreads by distinctive boot-lace rhizomorphs to attack any living tree or shrub. The honey-coloured fruiting bodies are distinctive and recognizable. Especially damaging to young trees, it has a wide variety of victims (the RHS has an extensive list online). There is currently no safely effective method of control except the immediate removal of all infected material, including a 45cm (18in) trench of soil around the affected area.
Leaf spot	This can either be a bacterial or fungal infection causing spots with yellow margins and white, black or brown centres. The infection most often occurs because the plant has not had the correct husbandry – usually too much or too little of a vital element. Invariably leaf spots are a sign that the gardener has been doing something wrong. Increase light, check the watering regime and improve ventilation. Remove all infected leaves and, if too bad, remove plant.
Mildew	Mildews occur on plants growing in very damp environments or, conversely, if they have prolonged hot weather and poor watering. Parasitic organisms, they coat the leaves of affected plants in a downy grey substance. The growth obstructs light and may cause the leaves to die after first withering or curling. Lower humidity and increase ventilation or increase watering of susceptible plants where needed.

Table 7 *continued*

Moulds and *Phytophthora*	Moulds come in two categories: minor and major. The minor species are generally caused by creatures like aphids and scale insects secreting a sticky substance on to leaves. This encourages black or sooty moulds to grow, causing a black sheath to grow over the leaf surface. Unsightly rather than harmful, the amount of light reaching the plant is reduced to the point of a reduction in photosynthesis. Using lukewarm water, wash away the mould. A second type of minor mould to look out for is found on the soil surface. Pasty white or grey in colour it can be a result of over-watering. Reduce your watering, remove as much of the soil as you can and replace with fresh, clean soil.
	A major pathogen is the genus *Phytophthora*, containing approximately 170 (so far known) plant-damaging fungus-like organisms in the mould family. They are one of the most important infections within the garden and wider commercial growing sectors and have the potential for catastrophic damage. Many are host-specific parasites, but a few such as *Phytophthora cinnamomi* will infect a wide range of plants from trees to commercial crops. The species causes root-rot or stem base decay and can live in the soil for many decades with no host plant in evidence. Difficult to control chemically, some are notifiable to government bodies.
Root rot	A variety of fungi cause root-rot in potted plants. Most commonly identified by the plant looking ill (i.e. leaves yellowing, wilting, poor growth or a bare stem). It will also show signs of chronic under-watering causing the gardener to exacerbate the problem by watering more. If root-rot is suspected, remove the plant from the pot and inspect the roots. They will look shrivelled, discoloured or pulpy. Both the plant and the soil will have the tell-tale smell of fungus. Cut off all affected roots to healthy growth, gently shake off all soil from the plant and remove all soil from the growing area. Replant in a new area or pot with fresh, sterilized soil.

ABOVE LEFT: Fungus growing on fruit in a tropical house. The conditions provided are perfect for a huge range of fungi and bacteria to thrive, so hygiene and ventilation are vital.

ABOVE MIDDLE: Canker on a mature *Prunus*. Until tested, it is unknowable whether it is bacterial or fungal.

ABOVE RIGHT: Peach leaf curl. A fungus spread in rain/water drops, it is difficult to eradicate without protecting the tree.

Table 8 Common infections – bacterial

Bacterial infections	Single-celled organisms, bacteria have existed on planet Earth for far longer than any other current kingdom, except perhaps viruses. Though they are relatively common in humans and animals, they are quite rare in plants. Lacking chlorophyll, they are dependent on the host for food, or on dead organic matter. Some groups of bacteria are beneficial or are essential to life, others cause disease. They are hard to treat, although some experiments with genetic editing of crops have bred in some resilience. Multitudinous in number, there are too many to mention here, so below is a list of possible infections that you may come across in your day-to-day gardening that are more serious. Poor or abnormal growth can be a sign of infection, but it is difficult to discern a difference between bacterial, viral, fungal or physiological disorders. Generally, the best advice is that, due to the nature of infection being inside a plant cell, sprays are ineffective. Destroy affected plants and cleanse the area thoroughly. Above all, do not save any seed.
Fireblight (*Erwinia amylovora*)	A notifiable disease, mainly affecting plants of the Rosaceae family, it is highly contagious. This includes species such as raspberry, apple, rose, pyracantha and cotoneaster. First signs include a sudden withering and dying of branches, blossoms, twigs, leaves. Very susceptible plants appear as if they have been scorched by a fire. Treatments are difficult once the infection has taken hold, but a preventative is thought to be the common antibiotic *Streptomycin*, which used as a spray, has been shown to prevent infection – however, as stated elsewhere, overuse of chemicals will breed resistance.
Canker (bacterial)	A disease primarily concerning *Prunus* and related plants, it affects the stems and leaves of the host plant. It causes 'shotholes' in the leaves and open weeping sores on the branches. If the infection spreads, the plant will die quickly. It must be noted here that sap oozing from *Prunus* is not uncommon and can be the result of damage or environmental stress. The best way to tell is to inspect the area, looking for sunken, dead areas in spring and early summer. Control is by religiously pruning out all affected areas in July and August, when the sap is not rising and tissues are most resistant. Clean your tools thoroughly after each cut, using a 70 per cent alcohol spray.
Xylella fastidosa	A very serious, notifiable disease, this pathogen infects approximately 600 different species of hosts, including olive, *Quercus, Ulmus, Acer, Platanus, Juglans, Eucalyptus, Salix, Prunus, Vitis, Citrus* and *Solanum.* (Also many herbaceous and commercial plants including, *Pelargonium, Brassica* and *Chenopodium.*) Spread by several insects that feed via the xylem, including the common froghopper (*Philaenus spumarius*). Symptoms include leaf scorch, wilt, dieback and plant death, but a difficulty arises in that they are almost identical to signs of drought, frost damage or establishment sickness. So far the UK has escaped this disease, but it is now so widespread in Europe that it is estimated it will be inadvertently imported. Any discovery will potentially lead to all host plants within 100m being destroyed and an 8km (5-mile) radius movement ban on all plants. Buy all plants from recognized and certified sources, making sure that adequate plant passports are in place. For more information, *go to*: http://www.confor.org.uk/media/246789/9-things-you-need-to-know-about-x-fastidiosa.pdf or https://www.xfactorsproject.eu/

Viruses are spread quite rapidly and in a multitude of ways. For example, they may be carried from one plant to another on dirty secateurs, on hands, on seed or by vectors such as aphids. It may be impossible to control the infection once it has established – meaning that the entire crop has to be removed and destroyed – though there have been some successes with inoculation, whereby a weak strain of the virus is introduced meaning that the plant creates antigens that prevent further attacks of stronger strains. Therefore, if the crop is valuable, it is always worth investigating whether an inoculation is available – one example is tomato mosaic virus, which has been successfully trialled and is in common use.

Other examples of methods to clean stock of viruses are: heat treatment (where seeds undergo immersion in 42°C water for a certain time to destroy pests) and meristem culture (a time-consuming and somewhat expensive procedure where the tips or meristems that are considered disease-free are propagated in agar culture). By far the most exciting (and somewhat controversial) is the progress made with gene editing. Using what is known as the *de novo* mersitem method (a technique that sidesteps the need for tissue culture), developmental hormones and gene-editing reagents are introduced into somatic cells of whole plants. This induces the meristems that then go on to produce shoots containing DNA modifications. These enhanced genes become permanent and are then passed on to future generations.

Be Warned

Ultimately, control of viruses for both the amateur and professional is difficult. Lift and burn diseased stock when symptoms are first noticed. If the problem is serious, control the various sucking insects that may be acting as vectors; this may be via predators (*see* Chapter 9) or, in exceptional circumstance, chemical. Buy certified plants from suppliers. Make sure that plants have 'plant passports' if imported.

A wasp. Not all 'pests' are pests. Wasps are important pollinators, as well as harvesting a great deal of aphids and other problem insects.

CHAPTER 9

ALLIES AND ALLIANCES

> 'The opportunity to secure ourselves against defeat lies in our own hands'
>
> Sun Tzu, Chinese military strategist, fifth century BCE

It is of benefit to the gardener to know their allies within the garden so that any pest species can be managed naturally. Where there is no natural predator or antidote, it is always worth seeking the advice of the related government departments – some species are notifiable under the law and should be reported immediately upon discovery. (A full list can be found at DEFRA https://planthealthportal.defra.gov.uk/pests-and-diseases/pest-and-disease-alerts/.) It is also a benefit for the gardener to understand the life cycle of both pest species and predators in order to understand how to keep numbers to a manageable level within the growing environment.

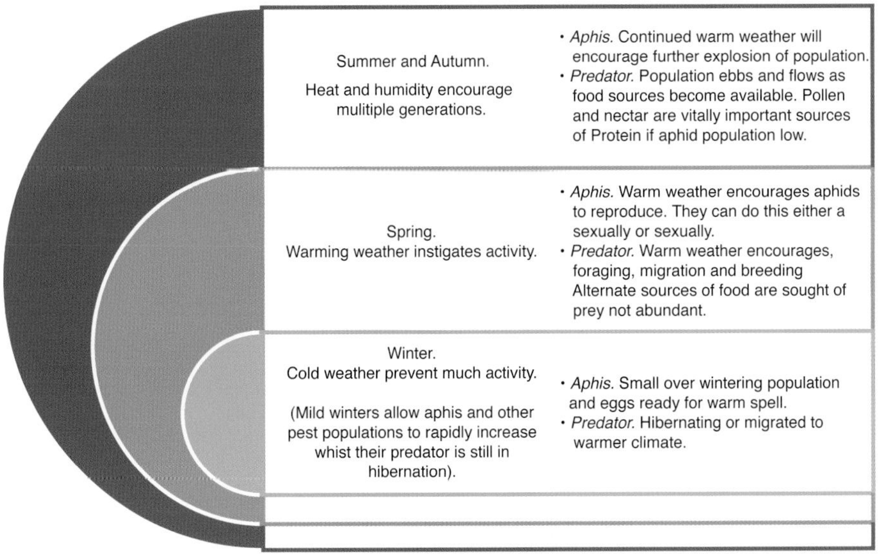

The relationship between *Aphis* and predator.

Round. Excellent for topiary, but exposure to strong winds or shade reduces viability.

Square with point. An ideal hedge for exposed sites. Can be shaped (as in diagram) to exposed side.

Triangle. Some use in areas where snow is an issue. Can be unduly thin on exposed side.

Square. Possibly the most common 'neat' hedge. Attractive and utilitarian.

Trapezium. A good shape for exposed sites. Flat top an issue in areas of heavy snow.

Hedges don't necessarily need to be pruned or shaped, but they can become unkempt and harbour disease. Always check at the stem, along the branches and under leaves for pest and disease. Depending on your situation, the shape is important. In areas with high snowfall, it is better to prune to prevent the snow from sitting atop. In areas of high wind, a more aerodynamic or 'open' shape may suit. Do not always assume a hedge should be cut with a mechanical hedge-cutter, as this method can sometimes encourage disease. Always think of how the hedge could be damaged and thus cause infection. Image based on information from the Tree Council.

Remember, it is of utmost importance to follow health and hygiene practices closely to reduce liability further. An extensive study, carried out in *Fruit Crop Ecology and Management* by Larry Gut, Annemiek

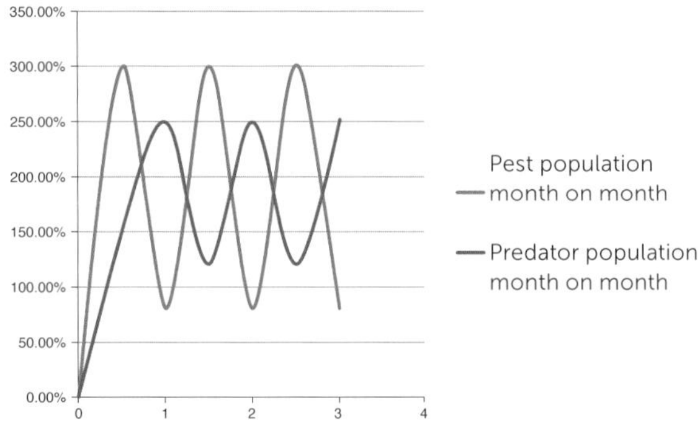

Populations of insect predators and prey (the numbers are arbitrary and do not refer to specific species).

LEFT: An area reserved for wildlife is highly beneficial to any garden. Corrugated iron is an excellent place for lizards or snakes to warm quickly, or to hide. The choice of flora, including nettles (*Urtica dioica*), is important food for the nettle aphid (which ladybirds feed on early in the season) and certain butterflies, including the peacock.

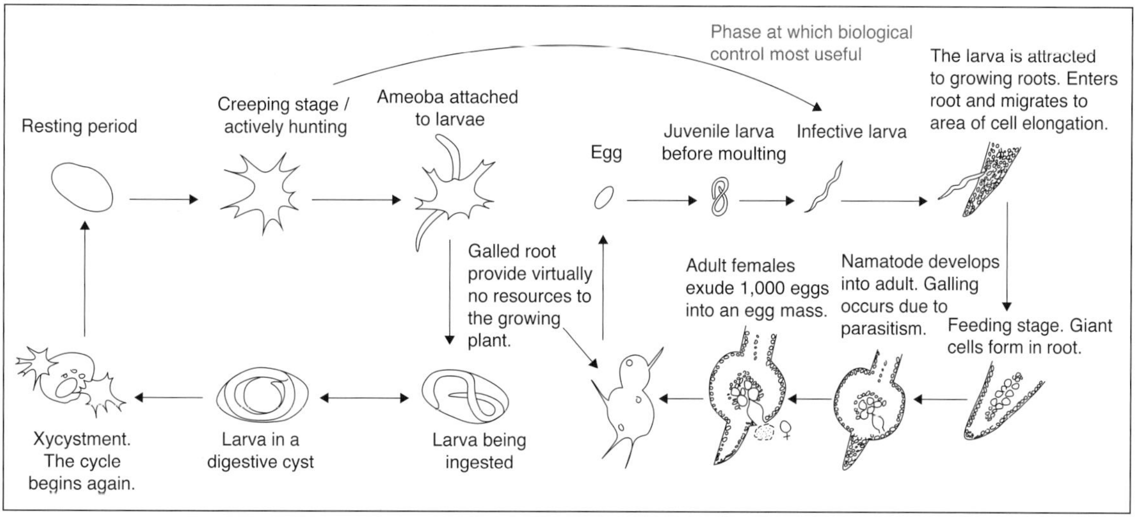

The life cycles of predator and prey. The complexity of life cycles means that there are often only narrow windows to address problems correctly. Each pest will have a predator, so once you have established what pest you have, consult a specialist to ascertain the best method of attack.

Schilder, Rufus Isaacs and Patricia McManus at Michigan State University, explores the idea that monitoring not only the pest species, but the predator species is vital to any method:

> A good scouting program is key to making ecologically sound pest management decisions. The need for control and the impact of any action are determined by monitoring pest and natural enemy populations. Sampling provides information on the organisms present, their stages of development, population densities, and the ratio of pests to natural enemies. A scout must know how an organism develops because different life stages may be monitored in different ways.... Sampling for predators and parasitoids is as important as monitoring pest populations. Higher pest densities can be tolerated when populations of natural enemies are also high. For example, a mite spray may be warranted in apple when there are two or three mites per leaf if there are no natural enemies, but a grower might wait until there are five or six per leaf if one predator mite per leaf is also present.

As with the pest species, it is of importance to know the predator's life cycle, so that it is provided with adequate food sources throughout the year – this may include nectar-bearing flowers or other invertebrates in order for it to remain. For example, predators of red spider mites often eat rust mites when its primary prey is not in evidence and parasitic wasps need a larval host for their young to overwinter. It is also important to understand life cycles in order to attract and maintain a healthy population of predators.

Horticultural Advice

The first port of call is usually the internet, but be aware that algorithms have a tendency to offer worse-case scenarios first, so it is always useful to get hands-on local advice. Advisory services are available, e.g. The Royal Horticulture Society offers limited free advice to members. DEFRA and The Forestry Commission are approachable for specific concerns and will send out inspectors if required. Companies can also be found online (such as the Woodland Trust and ADAS) for the commercial sector.

Chemical Control vs Natural Remedies

There are now 500 species (the list is growing) on the planet that are highly resistant to many of our chemical

Nursery spider (*Pisaura mirabilis*). Effective predators in grasslands and nettle beds, they use speed and ambush to hunt, rather than the traditional web.

Ask an Expert

With biodiversity in decline globally, how important is the use of natural predators in a protective environment?

Incredibly important. At Glasnevin we have a comprehensive and active biological programme that has almost eliminated the use of pesticides under glass. We still have plants with persistent pest problems that have to be targeted with horticultural soaps and plant invigorators. The success of any biological pest-control system is based on accurate identification of the pest, correct identification of the control and the most efficient dispersal method for that control. Release of biologicals is aided by the fact that ventilation can be closed during release periods for certain controls.

Brendan Sayers, National Botanic Garden, Glasnevin, Ireland

controls (*Fruit Crop Ecology and Management*, 2002). Whilst some are plants, most of these species are invertebrates, which show the most remarkable resilience and adaptability. Problem species include Colorado potato beetle and red spider mite – a full list can be found at www.pesticideresistance.org. The two primary factors that create resistance are genetics and intensive use of the same pesticides until a resistance is noticed. Add to this the knowledge that widespread and indiscriminate use of chemicals harms beneficial insects that aid our food production or keep pests down (80 per cent of pollinating insects are species other than bees). It is therefore necessary that extensive training and certification is required by law for many chemicals. Be advised, whilst chemical companies have a long list of dangers to look out for before a product comes to market, the mixing of chemicals and any resultant interactions or hybridization is not tested. In addition, tests are not carried out for such things as long-term cognitive change, or damage to the human biome – therefore it is sensible to assume that if a chemical kills via certain pathways, it will most certainly have an effect on helpful microbes in your gut that follow the same pathways (there is ongoing evidence-based research that proves a reduction in the stomach biome can cause cancer, a build-up in beta-amyloids or other debilitating diseases). According to one study:

> The bidirectional communication between the central nervous system and the gut microbiota plays a pivotal role in human health. Increasing numbers of studies suggest that the gut microbiota can influence the brain and behavior of patients. Various metabolites secreted by the gut microbiota can affect the cognitive ability of patients diagnosed with neurodegenerative diseases.
>
> Giau et al. (2018)

Inadvertent Introduction of Invasive Antagonists

Following several disasters where species were released into new environments (such as the rabbit, grey squirrel and harlequin beetle), great care is now taken to ensure no such repeat is made. Any introductions you may make in order to eradicate problems will have implications. It is against the law to introduce

Warning

You are legally obliged to understand the law when it comes to using chemicals. It is against the law for a contractor to spray or use chemicals (whether they are marked for domestic use or professional) if they do not possess the correct training on public and private land that is not theirs. It is also against the law to use chemicals no longer allowed under statute. It is the law that all chemicals are stored in a safe place. Hazardous chemicals, such as pesticides, fumigants and fungicides, must be under lock and key, in a separate area to other chemicals, such as fertilizers. They cannot be carried in a car or other vehicle in the same environment as the occupier. It must also be noted that large-scale storage of certain chemicals requires certification and a licence. All chemicals must be disposed of via a legally responsible method. Read labels carefully and thoroughly. Do not over-use chemicals or spray on to plants that you intend to use as food. Mix them accurately, making sure to dispose of any surplus in the correct manner and never into the drains or water supply. Always wear the correct protective equipment, treating the chemical with extreme care.

species that have not first been cleared for use by the appropriate authorities, so any purchases *must* be through recognized sources.

Organic vs Non-Organic: the future

There are currently two schools of thought. Those that follow the artificial chemical dogma and those that choose the 'organic path'. In both fields of thought, technology is moving forward apace, artificial intelligence (AI) and robot-controlled environments are becoming the norm across much of industry – which is no bad thing. A carefully crafted machine can assess the climate at a far faster rate than a layperson, though it is still currently a human that makes the final decisions. On an alternate track, there are ongoing trials using AI and lasers to eradicate weeds and pests in the commercial glasshouse environment – obviously, in some instances a monoculture can have benefits of simplification when constructing computer software but this often proves to be a circular argument.

On the domestic front, the responsibility still rests firmly with the gardener. First, understand that monocultures often prove to be less resilient and more prone to disease. Taking into consideration all that's been gained in the history of growing, it is well to remember Sun Tzu's key strategies (*see* Helpful Hint) and apply them to ideas that have been learned over years of trial and error. In a gardening context, these are as follows: understand the purpose of the space; understand the growing conditions; understand the factors you do not have control over; understand your methodology; be clear in your approach.

The Future: Natural Genetic Mutations vs Man-Made

With the implications of the Anthropocene not yet fully understood, life and how it evolves is under a great deal of stress. Therefore, many are looking to science to solve the issues some are noting in their day-to-day work. The scientist is now able to breed into plants certain qualities they desire (such as shorter, sturdier stems, disease resistance or heavier crops). They are also able to predict, and perhaps solve, the problems that arise when a weed becomes immune to herbicides or change fruiting times to fit shorter growing cycles. Thus we have turned to manipulating genetic traits within a plant's DNA to allow the farmer to control the pest species without harming the cash crop. This process has proved controversial and is unpopular amongst many consumers, but the problems mentioned are a global concern. Via CRISPR gene editing, a crop can be bred to be more resistant to pest attack. An example is the ToBRFV IR (brown rugose fruit virus), which is a major threat to *all* tomato production under glass. Whilst no danger to humans, if allowed to spread, ToBRFV IR will affect all known varieties of tomato, destroying entire crops. Currently, strict quarantine and hygiene is instigated at the first sign of attack (it can be spread via equipment, hand-tools, hands, soil and water). Companies such as Bayer have thus far been effective in gene editing new

Traditional methods of plant breeding include the introduction of several genes including (hopefully) the desired gene. This may also include unwanted traits and genes.

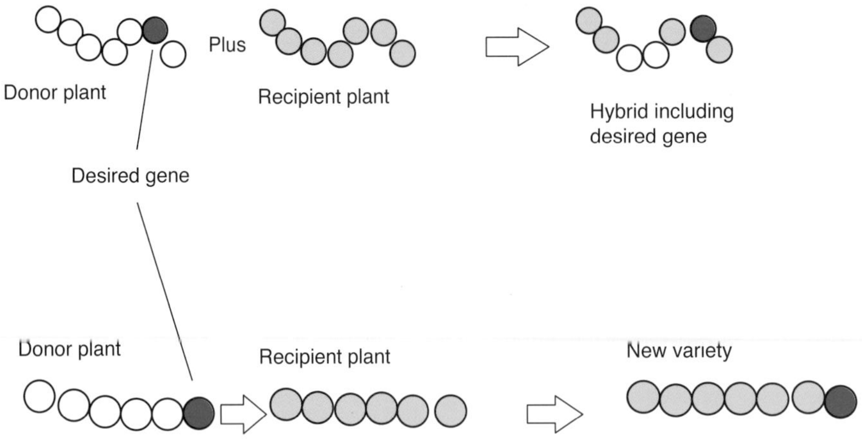

Genetic engineering enables the introduction to the plant of the required DNA without the need to include unwanted characteristics.

The principles of genetic and traditional breeding methods based on information published by US Food and Drug Administration. There is controversy surrounding such methods, as the results are not always positive, so many trials are carried out before introduction to ascertain issues.

varieties of tomatoes – successes having been recorded via new varieties that do not show the symptoms (even though affected), saving a globally important food.

However, genetic manipulation and chemical controls, whilst a useful tool, may not be the only way forward. According to experiments conducted by both NASA and MIT, the inherent risks associated with modern industrial horticulture are not a given, requiring massive investment in chemicals. So far, their research has offered an alternative (though less cost-efficient), proving that plants can be produced on an industrial scale utilizing natural behaviours within the plant's own physiology.

Helpful Hint

Using Sun Tzu's theories in the garden, follow his vital words, 'Strategy without tactics is the slowest route to victory' – therefore, it is always useful to stand in your space and ask yourself the following questions:

- Is it sensible to destroy all insect or invertebrate life when seeking to destroy one or two 'pests'? Are we missing an opportunity to use our allies? Are we inadvertently breeding stronger and fitter enemies? What is the outcome of using one single method of control?
- Is the space suited to our needs or are the pests utilizing our weaknesses? Can we mulch if the growing conditions just add more problems? Is there enough light? Is the temperature or humidity at an optimum? Is the sun an issue?
- Are we making our soil the best it can be for making our plants healthy? Are we creating frost pockets or areas of no air movement that will aid disease?
- Do we understand the garden or growing area? Have we read everything we possibly can to learn our art in the detail it deserves?
- Learn about your garden or growing environment. Use 'be prepared' as your mantra.

Companion Planting

This idea of planting 'companions' to reduce harm to a crop or plant is not new and has been backed by modern scientific method. It is always beneficial to understand what the planting of companions actually does. Some, such as *Tagetes*, will produce a chemical in the soil that repels wire worms and other soil-borne pests. Other plants will act as a mask – planting leeks with carrots will hide the carrot from the carrot-root fly and to some extent the leek moth from the leek (planting in a raised border will also negate pest attack in this instance). A third type of plant, such as marigold, will provide a rich source of nectar or pollen for predatory insects such as syrphid flies.

> Where natural enemies have access to pollen and nectar, there is often more predation and lower abundance of pests. Similarly, parasitic wasps supplement their diets by feeding on nectar, aphid honeydew, and other sources of sugar.
>
> Gut et al. (2002)

Within your garden, it is profitable – though time-consuming – to experiment with plants in order to understand your local flora and fauna. There is no point in seeking success with a companion plant that is designed to attract a predator of chalk downland if you are surrounded by acid moorland. Follow Sun Tzu's strategy and understand your terrain.

Also, following Sun Tzu's process, it is good to understand the strategy of deception. There are various plants that will hide or dissuade a pest attack, some of which are listed in Table 9. Be aware, some pests, such as birds and rabbits, will experiment before leaving a crop.

The marigold. An excellent annual flower that will seed freely in areas if it is protected from the hoe.

The walled garden at Goodnestone Park, Kent. The early seedlings are protected from birds and inclement weather by use of fleecing. Companion planting is also utilized where necessary.

Equally, plants can react strongly to being placed next to other plants: sometimes in a positive way, sometimes with negative consequences. The following table contains an idea of these companion plantings and probable adverse reactions for the vegetable area. Favourable plantings are in green, those that show adverse reaction are in red. Unfortunately no such list exists thus far for the wider garden.

Plant Allies

There is something to be said for understanding the symbiotic relationship between plant species. Recent research conducted first by Stanford University and then by Purdue University has shown that the healthy forest is a network of species, which include fungi, nitrogen-fixing bacteria and mosses. Maps published by the Global Forest Biodiversity Initiative show that many of these species share food between each other, providing an important balance. If one extends this research to the man-made garden, it is logical to conclude that plants within this setting have equal relationships. Equally, some plants have an unintended benefit to the gardener. Chicory (*Cichorium intybus*) and wild parsnip (*Pastinaca sativa*), to name just two examples, are excellent plants for breaking up subsurface pans due to their extended tap root. The foxglove (*Digitalis* spp.) is an excellent companion plant in both a woodland setting and the garden border – their extensive roots encourage other plants by their ability to store nutrients, but also keep the soil open and aerated. Nitrogen-fixing plants, such as sweet pea, lupin or runner bean, when planted in a border or hedge are excellent at keeping other plants healthy.

Invertebrate Allies

Insects and Arachnids

There are a multitude of insects that have been labelled as 'pests'. Notwithstanding, there are also a host of invertebrates that are a boon to have in the garden, many are insects – all of which are equally affected by insecticides. The ten most important predatory members of the

Table 9 Companion planting

Fennel	**Attracts:** predatory insects.
Urtica (nettles)	**Attracts:** ladybirds needing a supply of early spring food, such as nettle aphids.
Artemisia spp. Dried leaves scattered also.	**Repels:** birds.
Sage	**Repels:** carrot fly and onion moth.
Nasturtium	**Deters:** whitefly and cucumber beetle. **Traps:** aphids. **Attracts:** predatory insects.
Oregano	**Repels:** cabbage moth.
Leeks	**Repels:** carrot fly.
Marigold	**Repels:** whitefly (*Tagetes*). Kills nematodes. **Attracts:** predatory insects such as hoverfly.
Garlic	**Repels:** aphids, whitefly, some beetles, carrot fly, various root flies.
Wild garlic (can be invasive so advisory needed)	**Repels:** rabbit.
Chrysanthemums	**Repels:** beetles
Buddleia	**Attracts:** predatory insects, such as hoverfly.
Mint (dried leaves only as highly invasive)	**Repels:** flea beetle.
Wheat (until 15cm high, then carefully remove)	**Attracts:** wire worm. It is said that if you plant wheat, the wire worm will prefer the roots of wheat and will sit around them in preference. Carefully remove the plant from the border with the surrounding soil to reduce the population.
Dill	**Repels:** spider mites and aphids. **Attracts:** predatory wasp.

Allium Family	Legume Family	Brassica Family	Poacae Family (Corn)	Spinach and other leaves	Tomato
Brassica	Brocolli	Legume	Legumes	Brassica	Alliums
Lettuce	Carrot	Lettuce	Cucubrits	Lettuce	Legumes
Strawberry	Corn	Dill	Dill	Legumes	Nasturtium
Tomato	Lettuce	Carrots	Sunflower	Strawberry	Brassica
Carrot	Cucumber	Nasturtium	Tomato	Marigold	Corn
Beans	Pea	Spinach			Dill
Peas	Tomato	Sage			
	Onions	Thyme			
	Garlic	Rosemary			
	Leeks	Chard			
	Popporc	Sqaush			
	Marigold	Tomato			
		Peppers			
		Strawberry			

A table of favourable planting.

It is always of benefit to the gardener to understand the local microclimate and protective conditions. This is an avocado tree (*Persea americana*) growing well and fruiting (throughout the year) in Fulham, West London. As the climate changes to more favourable growing conditions, more exotic fruit will be able to grow unhindered outside, whereas other fruit that requires cold (such as apple), will move further north. However, that also means more exotic pests will be prevalent too! *Go to* https://planthealthportal.defra.gov.uk/pests-and-diseases/ on a regular basis for information.

The hoverfly is recognizable in gardens throughout the late spring, summer and early autumn. Plants with high nectar and pollen stores will encourage it into your garden. They are territorial; aerial battles are a common sight, as the males try to establish a domain.

Arthropod phylum are: centipedes (*Chilopoda*), ground beetles (carabids), rove beetles (Staphylinidae), assassin bugs (Reduviidae), ladybirds (Coccinellidae), wasps (Vespidae), hoverflies (Syrphidae), net-winged insects (Neuroptera) and dragonflys (Anisoptera). Though not insects, arachnids (spiders, including mites) also play an important part in pest elimination within the garden setting.

Much has been said of clearing the garden of detritus and mess, which is logical in many senses. However, in order to attract the predatory insects, one needs some latitude in thinking. Bug hotels are an excellent method of providing shelter, so too wood piles and areas of wild for overwintering purposes. Many spiders will come into the home to overwinter, so progress with some thought before destroying them. Ladybirds will need an area to cluster and hibernate. Depending on the age of the house, these can include the gaps in windows and rolled curtains. Queen wasps and queen hornets also find house warmth a useful winter roost, so be aware of similar spaces in spring when they reawaken.

Molluscs

It is generally thought that molluscs, such as slugs and snails, are only a pest in the garden, indeed many websites dedicate themselves to identifying only the 'pests' with no thought to identifying the thirty or so varieties

A seven-spot ladybird travels across a leaf in search of prey in late March. Typically hibernating in hollow plant stems, any spell of warmth early in the year will wake the ladybird from its slumber, so it is good for the garden to have a wild area where nettles grow to supply an early crop of food for these vital insect predators.

BELOW: A bug hotel can be a fun distraction for children in the garden and helps them to understand the wider biodiversity.

of mollusc one may find in the garden (some extremely rare). However, there are species that actively hunt other molluscs. Depending on your soil, site and situation, these can be abundant.

The leopard slug (*Limax maximus*), distinctive for its markings, is quite common and will actively hunt other snails or slugs. Another is the ghost slug (*Selenochlamys ysbryda*), which will eat both slugs and earthworms. Whilst there are species of flatworm and nematodes that cause havoc in the soil – eating roots, tubers and shoots – there is also a wide variety of species that are predatory, eating slugs and other nematodes or flatworms.

Table 10 Helpful insects and arachnids (arthropods)

Centipedes (Chilopoda)	An excellent, many-legged garden predator. Found in the soil surface or roaming through leaf piles or compost heaps.
Ground beetles (carabids)	A fast and voracious hunter of slugs. Several species exist. One of the gardener's most useful allies. Sadly drowns in traps just as easily as slugs, so raise the slug traps slightly higher to prevent inadvertent issues.
Beetles (Staphylinidae)	Not all beetles are damaging to plants. Some are useful hunters, ridding the garden of troublesome species. Woodpiles and bug hotels are excellent hiding places.
Assassin bugs (Reduviidae)	Fast-moving ground predators, these bugs need sources of nectar or pollen when protein is scarce.
Ladybirds (Coccinellidae)	A voracious predator of aphids. Both its larval and adult stages are useful in the garden. They like to overwinter in houses or hollow trees and woodpiles.
Wasps (Vespidae)	A great ally. The European hornet is an essential predator of woodland gardens and should not be feared as it is quite shy. (If Asian hornet is seen, the authorities should be notified immediately.) Smaller wasps will predate many pest species.
Hoverflies (Syrphidae)	A large family of predatory flying insects, not all have the characteristic striped carapace. They have complex food requirements depending on stage of development, including nectar and pollen. Some species migrate from warmer climates for the summer only.
Net-winged insects (Neuroptera)	Lace-wings and other similar insects are equal to ladybirds in their appetite for aphids. Best released in large numbers. They overwinter in houses, crevices and hollow trees.
Dragonflys (Anisoptera)	Living only a short while as adults, they are fast-moving. These predators dominate the pond and garden alike. Their young live in ponds or rivers for several years, so be careful what chemicals are added.
Spiders (arachnids, including mites)	An exceptional ally to have in the home and in the garden. All UK species are harmless to humans; however, be aware of introduced species such as the 'false widow', which can have a nasty bite. Mites are the smaller cousins of spiders. Some are destructive but it is worth noting that there are many predatory species that can be bought and introduced to the growing space, if needed as an effective control.

Helpful Hints

Whilst it is useful to know what pest is doing what and where, it is also useful to understand the full life-cycle of that pest in order fully to comprehend how to eradicate the problem. For example, whilst releasing a predatory mite such as *Amblyseius andersoni* into a greenhouse to control spider mites, young thrips, rust mites and so on, as described, it will be of no benefit if the pest species is at the wrong stage of its life cycle. This may seem like a lot of work for a pest that was once simply eradicated by the use of a chemical. However, like the antibiotic resistance in human pathogens, chemicals must now only be used as a last resort to prevent further genetic tolerance being inbred and causing a much more serious problem.

Table 11 Helpful molluscs, nematodes and flatworms

Molluscs (Limacidae and Trigonochlamydidae)	There are two useful predatory molluscs in the UK (so far discovered). The leopard slug (*Limax maximus*) and the ghost slug (*Selenochlamys ysbryda*). Both hunt other slugs and snails. NB If you are thinking of introducing foreign species to your garden for specific purposes, you must first speak with DEFRA.
Flatworms (Geoplanidae)	Useful flatworms are generally introduced to the garden via drenches. These animals seek out their prey in the soil. Knowing the life cycle of the intended prey is important. Be aware, some flatworm chemical treatments include the use of heavy metals, which may have a long-term detrimental effect on your soil.
Nematodes	A phylum of over 25,000 species, many unclassified. An exceptionally useful predator, they are sometimes already present in the soil, but for specific infestations, they can be introduced into the garden via drenches. The instructions must always be followed to make sure the process will have effect. Knowing the life cycle of the both the predator and prey is vital.

The leopard slug (*Limax maximus*). A greatly misunderstood ally.

Vertebrate Allies

Amphibians and Reptiles

It is generally thought that amphibians, such as frogs and toads, need a pond. This is true only during the breeding season. The majority of time they will spend out of the water in areas not affected by the direct sun, foraging for invertebrate food such as worms, slugs, flatworms and insects. Newts require a different habitat, preferring to remain in the water, generally at the bottom of the pond in mud or silt build-up or amongst vegetation. They require areas to hide in winter, especially dry stone walls or log piles from which, in warmer spells, they can forage.

Reptiles need areas to bask in the sun, areas to lay their eggs (most usefully warm piles of leaves or compost bins), areas to hunt such as long grass and areas to overwinter. Large, flat rocks or log piles in the sun with a snug space underneath are commonly most useful for them, though a corrugated iron sheet that sees the sun is also a most welcome home.

Avian

Birds are a complex issue within the garden biome. Many will eat seedlings, or pick at verdant young growth and flower buds. Other birds will destroy a row of cabbages by ripping at the leaves or dig up the lawn in order to get at a pest species like 'leather-

Table 12 Helpful amphibians and reptiles

Frogs (Ranidae)	A great insectivore and slug eater. Need an area to hibernate.
Toads (Bufonidae)	Like the frog, they need water to breed. They need leaf piles to hibernate or just under the soil in untidy borders.
Newts (Salamandridae)	These animals are partially aquatic, coming out at night to hunt slugs and insects. They overwinter in cracks in walls or under stones.
Common lizard (*Zootoca vivipara*)	The UK's most common lizard, it has a wide range of habitats from grassland to woodland. They are fast-moving insectivores. Provide a place of shelter as they are prey animals.
Grass snake (*Natrix natrix*)	An excellent predator, they will eat small animals as well as insects and slugs. Ideally, they need long grass and are aquatic.
Slow worm (*Anguis fragilis*)	Insectivore and molluscivore, they are actually legless lizards. Like to be hidden, as they fall prey to cats.
Smooth snake (*Coronella austriaca*)	Another species of legless lizard, restricted to the sandy heathland areas of the West.

jacket' grubs – much to the annoyance of the gardener. The gardener must protect their crop before this happens, not curse the bird for their own laziness. In the case of the leatherjackets and other grubs, nematodes can be employed, but once the damage is done, there is little to do but reseed. This may be of benefit to the gardener as the lawn may have needed relaying anyway.

It is always the role of the gardener to understand the wider biodiversity at stake. A rose chafer grub may be a nuisance, but both young and adult are a good food source for birds and other useful predators. Those birds, like the robin and tits, remain all year and will eat caterpillars, greenfly and other insects that they find as you tend the garden. The song thrush and its relative, the blackbird, will happily rid your garden of slugs and snails. Raptors too, especially the smaller types such as the migratory merlin, will eat flying insects. Other migratory species, such as swallows, martins, swifts and wagtails, eat vast amounts of insects for the short few months that they grace our skies.

Mammal

Whilst it is accepted that small mammals can be a problem, especially mice, rabbits and rats, other mammals such as foxes, hedgehogs, stoats, weasels and

Bird boxes are a good addition to any wildlife-friendly garden, but they must be handled carefully (to avoid human scent). They must be designed well for the species you are aiming to attract, also constructed well to stop predation from animals, such as grey squirrels. Lastly, they must be placed in a spot appropriate to the species, making sure they are not liable to 'cook' in the full heat of the sun.

Table 13 Helpful avians

Robin (*Erithacus*)	A familiar bird to many gardens, it is a member of the flycatcher family. It is an excellent insectivore and a welcome friend, often following the gardener about. They like to nest in specific areas and are fussy about nest boxes, so consult the RSPB or simonkingwildlife.com
Treecreeper (Certhiidae)	Seen more in wooded gardens, this useful and lively bird will hop up a tree finding insect pests. They like to nest in hollow trees.
Nuthatch (Sittidae)	A bird of wooded gardens, this light-blue tinted bird walks down the tree hunting for its insect prey. Chatty birds, a loud song demarks their territory. Nest in hollow trees or specialist nest boxes.
Tits (Paridae)	A wide variety of small birds, they hunt in large family groups. Specific nest boxes can be purchased.
Thrushes (Turdidae)	Usually solitary birds, they have small territories in the garden, hunting slugs and snails. Their song is quite distinctive. Nesting habits vary but include sheds and quiet areas of outbuildings.
Dunnock (Prunellidae)	A small, shy bird similar in appearance to sparrows, they are voracious insectivores. As the common name (hedge sparrow) suggests, they need thickets or dense hedging to nest.
Firecrest and goldcrest (Regulidae)	Tiny birds, weighing 3g. Highly active, they are great insectivores. They nest in thickets.
Wagtail (Motacillidae)	Familiar to many with their ever-bobbing tail, some overwinter, others are summer visitors. All eat insects in large numbers. They nest in holes in walls or the abandoned nests of larger birds.
Wren (Troglodytidae)	A small bird with a loud voice! Excellent insectivores. They prefer to nest in walls, trees or similar boxes to tits or secluded spaces. They like to have overwinter roosts *en masse*.
Owls (Strigidae and Tytonidae)	The little owl is an excellent hunter of small animals and insects. The barn owl and tawny owl also hunt small mammals. Nest boxes are beneficial as many of their roosts have been converted into houses.
Warblers (Phylloscopidae)	Small birds that you can hear, but rarely see. Excellent insectivores, they have varying habitats, roosts and nest requirements.
Swallows and martins (Hirundinidae)	Exceptionally beautiful flyers and important insectivores. Summer visitors only, they are becoming rarer due to human predation and lack of nesting sites. Their nests are distinctive. It is illegal to destroy or disturb a swallow nest.
Woodpeckers and wrynecks (Picidae)	Inquisitive yet shy, these birds add a splash of glamour and are excellent at finding pest insects. They nest in hollow trees.
Hobby, merlin and kestrel (Accipitridae)	Familiar members of the raptor family. The kestrel will hunt small mammals and insects. The hobbys and merlins are fast birds that migrate, but will hunt in the summer months in the UK.
Flycatcher (Muscicapidae)	A wonderful but rare summer visitor to the UK. Becoming more frequent as global temperatures warm.
Finches (Fringillidae)	An attractive bird family that is very omnivorous. Whilst they will eat insects such as caterpillars, they will happily eat young plants, seedlings and seeds. Varying nest boxes are available, but they prefer thickets and hedges.
Crows (Corvidae)	A highly intelligent group of birds, which include jackdaws, magpies, jays and rooks. Eighty per cent of their diet is insects, rodents and carrion. Though destructive in some instances, they are valuable predators in the garden.

Bat boxes are an excellent way of encouraging bats into your garden. Always consult your local bat conservation charity or wildlife trust before installing. Be aware bats are protected species, so once inhabited, it is illegal to move them without consent.

shrews will rid the garden of mice, rats, snails, slugs and other problem invertebrates. Bats are also immensely important in the garden biodiversity, being excellent insectivores. A good idea is to understand the requirements of the mammals you wish to encourage (including their roosting or nesting habits) and those you wish to discourage. The most important being that all require the dense cover of a well-established hedge to forage and escape larger predators.

A bee resting during a rain storm. With bees in decline globally, it is a common mistake to assume they all have the same life cycles. Some require soft sand in which to lay their eggs, others brickwork or wood. Some live only for a few days as an adult. Others live in hives, cuckoo (another species raising your young as their own) or are solitary. All require our help.

Other Considerations

Sadly, our persecution and eradication of larger indigenous predators, such as the golden eagle, the lynx and wolf, has seen a gradual increase of deer numbers. Add to this the introduction of alien species, such as the muntjac, an increase in damage is unsurprising. It is, therefore, best for the garden owner to build a deer- and rabbit-proof fence at the perimeter, rather than constantly fight remedial battles with an animal that rapidly adapts; but always be aware of the wider ecology.

Table 14 Helpful mammals

Fox (Canidae)	Though not popular, they are a member of the dog family; their smell often alerts the garden owner to their presence long before you see them. They will happily rid the garden of rats, mice and slugs.
Weasels and stoats (Mustelidae)	Superb hunters, more inclined to the countryside, they will eat insects and small mammals up to rabbit size. Owing to their diminutive size, they are hunted. Thus they prefer mature thick hedging to hunt in, though tunnels, pipes and rockeries are also favoured.
Hedgehogs (Erinaceidae)	Excellent enemies of slugs and snails, they are sadly becoming rarer due to traffic. From a population of 35 million, it is estimated there are now fewer than a million. They like hedges and leaf piles and large grass clumps to hibernate in winter. They are excellent climbers so will not be put off by a fence.
Bats (Chiroptera)	Superb animals to encourage into the garden via bat boxes or hollow trees; there are many species. Protected under law, any roosts should not be disturbed. These animals eat a huge amount of pest insects. Bat boxes for specific species can be purchased from the Bat Conservation or Wildlife Trusts.
Shrews (Soricidae)	Small mammals with an incredible appetite. Their average lifespan is a year, but in that time, they must eat their own bodyweight every day to survive. They will often make a nest in warm compost heaps.

GLOSSARY

Airflow The flow of air through a structure.

Alluvial A soil that has been unconsolidated by the action of water and redeposited in a non-marine setting (such as flood plain). Made up of clay, sand, grit and biological matter.

Anthropocene A proposed geological epoch. It dates from the first signs of significant human impact on the Earth's ecology and geology, including man-made climate change.

Beta-amyloids A brain protein thought to be a contributory factor in Alzheimer's.

Biologicals Insect predators.

Chlorosis Yellowing of leaves due to illness or nutrient deficiency in leaf.

CRISPR A genome editing technique, by finding specific genes and altering the DNA sequences.

DDT (dichlorodiphenyltrichloroethane) An organochlorine compound used in agriculture and horticulture as a pesticide.

Deciduous A woody plant that loses its leaves in winter to regrow them when the weather improves.

Evergreen A woody plant that remains in leaf all year round.

FAST Fruit Advisory Services Team.

Flocculation The process of changing the structure of clays into larger clumps known as 'flocs', using chemical processes.

Frost pockets An area where frost can be trapped by a retaining wall or hedge. Happens especially at the bottom of hills or in areas with little air movement.

Galvanized The application of zinc to a metal such as steel to protect it from rust.

Hard frost A situation when both the air and ground freeze.

Heave A problem created when subsoil movement cracks brickwork or concrete in an adverse way. Associated with subsidence.

Leaching A process of weathering where minerals and or nutrients are washed from soils or walls.

MDPE Medium density polyethylene.

Microbiota Microbes; small living organisms.

Microclimate The climate of a small or restricted area. One that differs from the wider surrounding area.

Natural colonization A natural process where plants are allowed to set seed, expand via root runs or layer from local sources, forming a larger colony or woodland.

NPK Nitrogen, phosphorus, potassium.

Offset pattern A pattern of planting where rows of plants are 'offset' in a diagonal formation similar to a W.

P&D Pest and disease.

Pan An impermeable hardening of the soil, either at the surface or below. Caused by a number of conditions, from weathering to mechanical interaction. The result can lead to water running off or waterlogging.

Pathogen A biological organism that can produce disease.

pH The scale in chemistry that measures the acidity or alkalinity of a substance.

Phytosanitary The health of plants, especially with regard to trade.

PPE Personal protective equipment.

Provenance The known history of something, be it manufactured or created.

Sitting wet A place where water does not evaporate by the sun's heat causes plants to sit wet.

Symbiosis A biological interaction between two different biological organisms within an ecosystem. It can be mutualistic, parasitic, predatory, competitive or commensal.

Syringing Watering using a hose or watering can with rose.

Thermostacially controlled Apparatus that automatically controls the temperature of a space.

Wind load A horizontal load placed on an exterior structure by the wind. Measured in kilograms per square metre.

BIBLIOGRAPHY

Anderson, J., Hespeler, E. and Zwiren, S., *Monocultures in America: A system that needs more diversity* (2017). https://blogs.umass.edu/natsci397a-eross/monocultures-in-america-a-system-that-needs-more-diversity/.

Beattie, W.R., *Hotbeds and Coldframes. US Department of Agriculture Farmers Bulletin No. 1743*, 1935

Beeton, I., *Mrs Beeton's Garden Management* (Wordsworth Reference, 2008)

Chesterman, J., Marten, M., May, J., et al., *An Index of Possibilities: Energy & Power* (Clanose Publishers, 1974)

Coleman, D., *Understanding Soil Processes: One of the Last Frontiers in Biological and Ecological Research* (University of Georgia, 2011)

Fletcher, C.R.L. and Kipling, R., *A History of England* (London: Henry Frowde and Hodder & Stoughton, 1911)

Giau, V.V., Wu, S.Y., Jamerlan, A., An, S.S.A., Kim, S.Y. and Hulme, J., Gut Microbiota and their Neuroinflammatory Implications in Alzheimer's Disease. *Nutrients*, 2018, Nov 14; 10(11): 1765. Doi: 10.3390/nu10111765. PMID: 30441866; PMCID: PMC6266223.

Griffith, S.B., *Sun Tzu: The Art of War* (Oxford University Press, 1963)

Gut, L., Schilder, A., Isaacs, R. and McManus, P., *Fruit Crop Ecology and Management* (Michigan State University Extension Bulletin E-2759, December 2002)

Hibberd, S., *The Amateur's Greenhouse and Conservatory* (Groombridge and Sons, 1873)

Hill, T., *The Gardener's Labyrinth* (Oxford University Press, 1987)

Illing, H.P.A., *Is Working in Greenhouses Healthy? Evidence Concerning the Toxic Risks that Might Affect Greenhouse Workers* (MRC Institute for Environment and Health, University of Leicester, 1997)

Kelway, C., *Seaside Gardening* (W.H. & L. Collingridge Ltd, 1962)

Kipling, R. 'The Glory of the Garden' in Fletcher, C.R.L. and Kipling, R. *A History of England* (Henry Frowde and Hodder & Stoughton, 1911)

Ledward, D., *The Idiot Gardener's Handbook* (Robson Books, 1987)

Leunenberger, M., Morris, J.M., Chan, A.M., Leonelli, L., Niyogi, K.K. and Fleming, G.R., *Dissecting and Modeling Zeaxanthin – and Lutein-Dependent Nonphotochemical Quenching in* Arabidopsis thaliana (Berkeley University, 2017)

Lloyd, C., *The Well-Tempered Garden* (Lyons Press, 1970)

Novak, M., Nikola Tesla's Amazing Predictions for the 21st Century (*Smithsonian Magazine,* 2013)

Opatowski, D., Wang, Y. and Ormsby, M., *Requirements for the Use of Fumigation as a Phytosanitary Measure,* (2014–04) (International Plant Protection Convention, 2018)

Reed, J., *Electrical Weed Control in Field Vegetables Project Number: Fv 346* (Silsoe Technology Ltd, November 2009)

Rothman, D.H., Thresholds of catastrophe in the Earth system. *Science Advances,* 2017, Sep; 3(9)

Singh, Dr R., *Plant Parasitic Nematodes: The Hidden Enemies of Farmers* (Bareilly College, 2015)

Stanley, J.M., *Electric Heating of Hotbeds* (Washington, DC: US Dept of Agriculture, 1964)

Sudell, R., *Secrets of Successful Gardening* (Odhams Press Ltd, 1933)

Tallack, J., *The Book of The Greenhouse* (J. Lane, 1901)

Tyler-Whittle, M., *Common or Garden* (William Heinemann Ltd, 1969)

Walkden, B., *Aids to Better Gardening* (David & Charles, 1973)

Watson, W., *The Gardener's Assistant* (The Gresham Publishing Company, 1925)

Willis, K., *Extinction: The Facts* (BBC Television, 2020)

Further Recommended Reading

Bird, R. and Kelly, J., *Alpines and Rock Garden Plants* (Ward Lock, 1998)

Bowen, L., *The Art and Craft of Growing Orchids* (B.T. Batsford Ltd, 1976)

Brady, N. and Weil, R., *Elements of the Nature and Properties of Soil* (Pearson Education Inc., 2004)

Bülow-Olsen, A., *Plant Communities* (Penguin Books, 1978)

Burton, J., *The Oxford Book of Insects* (Peerage Books, 1979)

Callahan, D., *Windows from Wood?* (2016) https://www.kth.se/en/aktuellt/nyheter/kth-forskare-har-uppfunnit-genomskinligt-tra-1.638511

Greenwood, P. and Halstead, A., *Pests and Disease* (RHS Dorling Kindersley, 2003)

Heiney, Anna, *Growing Plants in Space* (NASA, 2021)

Hellyer, A.G.L., *Amateur Gardening: Pocket Guide* (Collingridge Books, 1941)

Impelluso, L., *Gardens in Art* (Getty Publications, 2007)

Johnson, H., *The Principle of Gardening* (Mitchell Beazley Publishers Ltd, 1979)

Joyce, D., *The Complete Book of Greenhouse Gardening* (Marshall Cavendish Books Ltd, 1979)

Macmillan, H.F., *Tropical Planting and Gardening* (revised edition) (Macmillan & Co., 1991)

Nicholls, R., *The Plant Doctor* (Bantam Books, 1975)

Russell, Sir E., *A Student's Book of Soils and Manures* (Cambridge University Press, 1946)

Sackville West, V., *Garden Book* (Michael Joseph, 1968)

Salisbury, F.B. and Ross, C.W., *Plant Physiology* (Wadsworth Publishing Inc., 1992)

Smith, T., *Cleaning and Disinfecting the Greenhouse* (Greenhouse Crops and Floriculture Program – Retired, University of Massachusetts, Amherst, 2015)

Stokes, J. and Hand, K., *The Hedge Tree Handbook* (The Tree Council, 2005)

Titchmarsh, A., *Guide to Greenhouse Gardening* (Hamlyn Publishing, 1980)

Useful Web Links

DEFRA https://planthealthportal.defra.gov.uk/pests-and-diseases/pest-and-disease-alerts/

Greenhouses: Choosing. Royal Horticultural Society. https://www.rhs.org.uk/advice/profile?pid=449

NASA Light. https://www.nasa.gov/feature/goddard/2021/new-nasa-data-sheds-sun-light-on-climate-models/

NASA Glass From Space. https://www.nasa.gov/audience/forstudents/5-8/features/space_glass_feature.html

NASA Progressive Plant Growing is a Blooming Business 2007. https://www.nasa.gov/vision/earth/technologies/aeroponic_plants.html

www.pesticideresistance.org.

https://www.cropscience.bayer.com/innovations/seeds-traits/a/importance-plant-breeding

http://skepticwonder.fieldofscience.com/2010/08/sunday-protist-nematode-hunting-amoebae.html

INDEX